Discovering Fiction 2

A READER OF NORTH AMERICAN SHORT STORIES

2nd Edition

Judith Kay

Rosemary Gelshenen

CAMBRIDGE
UNIVERSITY PRESS

CAMBRIDGE
UNIVERSITY PRESS

32 Ave. of the Americas, New York, NY 10013-2473

Cambridge University Press is part of the University of Cambridge.

It furthers the University's mission by disseminating knowledge in the pursuit of education, learning and research at the highest international levels of excellence.

www.cambridge.org
Information on this title: www.cambridge.org/9781107622142

First Edition first published 2001
Second Edition published 2013
4th printing 2014

Printed in Mexico by Editorial Impresora Apolo, S.A. de C.V.

A catalog record for this publication is available from the British Library

ISBN 978-1-107-63802-0 Student's Book Introduction
ISBN 555-5-559-33268-0 Instructor's Manual Introduction
ISBN 978-1-107-65222-4 Student's Book 1
ISBN 555-5-559-21768-0 Instructor's Manual 1
ISBN 978-1-107-62214-2 Student's Book 2
ISBN 555-5-559-03087-6 Instructor's Manual 2

Art direction, book design, editorial management, and layout services: Hyphen S.A.
Cover images: Dougal Waters/Media Bakery; Kate Smyres/Cambridge University Press
Illustrations: Dan Brown: *A Day's Wait, The Last Leaf, The Lottery, The Circus;* Miles Hyman: *All Summer in a Day, Too Soon a Woman;* Lori Mitchell: *Thank You, Ma'm, Désirée's Baby, A Rice Sandwich;* Victor Moschopoulos (hyphen): *The Circuit, Thicker Than Water;* Rick Powell: *The One Day War, A Visit to Grandmother, The Warriors;* Alexis Seabrook: *The Third Level.*

To our parents, who would have been proud.

To our families and friends, who encouraged us.

To our students, who inspired us.

ABOUT THE AUTHORS

JUDITH KAY has extensive experience teaching writing, communication skills, and grammar. While teaching at Marymount Manhattan College in New York City, she met Rosemary Gelshenen. In addition to being colleagues, they started writing textbooks together. When Kay moved to Florida she taught at Lynn University in Boca Raton and Broward College in Broward County, Florida. Both Kay and Gelshenen have taught seminars in collaborative writing, and have presented workshops at regional and international meetings of TESOL.

Kay has a master's degree in TESOL from Hunter College and is a member of Phi Beta Kappa. She has published both short stories and poetry.

ROSEMARY GELSHENEN teaches literature, creative writing, and grammar in New York City at both Hunter College and New York University. She has also taught at Marymount Manhattan College, where she met Judith Kay. Formerly, she taught English at Norman Thomas High School and was a teacher trainer for the New York City Board of Education. Her awards include the Veritas Medal for Excellence in Education (1986) and New York City Teacher of the Year (1983). She also received two Impact II grants for innovative methods of teaching.

Gelshenen's articles on teaching methods have appeared in numerous educational publications, and she lectures on literary topics. She is the author of *Instant English Literature* (1994), a lighthearted approach to the lives and works of nineteenth-century English novelists.

CONTENTS

TO THE STUDENT

As our students progress in their study of English, we have found that they often ask us to recommend stories and novels. For this book, we chose outstanding short stories by American authors – stories that we particularly like and that our students, over the years, have enjoyed reading and discussing, and that we hope you will enjoy, too.

At this point in your study of English, you have a good command of the language: you understand a great deal; you speak easily and comfortably; and you write well-structured English sentences. However, even though you've come a long way, there are probably certain aspects of English that continue to cause problems.

No matter how well you read and write English, sometimes you're still not sure which prepositions to use and when to use an article. Irregular verbs continue to "bug" you, and of course, there are all those idioms. To reinforce your study of English, this textbook will review some of the grammar you have already learned.

Any study of a language should also include an exploration of its culture. Whether you are observing the California landscape of William Saroyan's story, the midwestern farm in Sherwood Anderson's tale, or the city streets of Langston Hughes's writing, you are seeing America. Through these stories, you will develop some additional insights into American culture as it has spanned the past two hundred years.

Enter the world of literature with us now, and savor the richness of the words, images, and characters you will meet.

JUDITH KAY
ROSEMARY GELSHENEN

TO THE INSTRUCTOR

After many years of teaching, we found no books that offered a combination of literature and grammatical review geared to meet the needs of the high-intermediate and advanced student. Though no book offers everything to the classroom instructor, we think our "offspring" comes close!

All the stories included in *Discovering Fiction* have been used successfully in our classes. The sections on Guessing Meaning from Context and Idioms and Expressions enable students to read the stories on their own at home. We have chosen a cross section of outstanding stories both for their style and content, so that students will appreciate the breadth of American literature.

The grammar exercises that follow each selection are addressed to the high-intermediate and advanced student. These exercises are meant to serve as a grammar review and reinforcement. Hopefully, they will help students overcome those elusive trouble areas – prepositions, articles, irregular verbs, and so forth. We have not arranged the grammar in order of difficulty. Therefore, you may assign the stories according to the needs of your students.

Suggestions for writing and discussion are also included in each chapter. We find that our students respond best to assignments that touch on their personal experiences – for example, writing about their own fears after reading Hemingway's "A Day's Wait." Many of the stories lend themselves to dramatization. This is an excellent way to encourage shy students to participate in class activities.

We hope the variety of selections will enable you to expand the literary horizons of your students. Many students have read Mark Twain and Ernest Hemingway, but few have been exposed to Langston Hughes, Ray Bradbury, or Shirley Jackson. These short stories are often a springboard to reading other stories and novels by the same authors. What better gift can we give our students than to encourage them to read?

JUDITH KAY
ROSEMARY GELSHENEN

HIGHLIGHTS

CHAPTER 1

A Day's Wait
ERNEST HEMINGWAY

A PREPARING TO READ

1 Think Before You Read

Answer the following questions:

1 What do you know about Ernest Hemingway's life and writings?
2 Which of his novels or short stories have you read?
3 What do you think the title of the story means?
4 What makes parents more or less sensitive to their children's fears?
5 Are parents always sensitive to their children's fears?
6 Why do children sometimes hide their fears from their parents?

4   A Life Lesson

THINK BEFORE YOU READ

Reflecting on the topic before reading helps students connect to the story.

---

2 Literary Term: Point of View

Eyewitnesses to accidents or crimes often describe what they saw in very different ways. People see situations from their own perspectives. In "A Day's Wait," Hemingway chose to write the narrative from the father's **point of view** (the "I" of the story). Imagine the events of the story from a different character's point of view.

3 Idioms and Expressions

You will find these idioms and expressions in the story:

got a headache had a pain in one's head	**made a note** wrote something down
took the boy's temperature used a thermometer to measure fever	**take it easy** relax
	we make we create

B THE STORY

About the Author

Ernest Hemingway (1899–1961) is a well-known writer whose works are read all over the world. Like Mark Twain, he is regarded as a representative American writer.

Born in a suburb of Chicago, Hemingway began writing in high school, and after graduation, he worked as a reporter. During World War I, Hemingway tried to join the army but was turned down because of his age. Instead, he volunteered as an ambulance driver for the Red Cross. In Italy, he was injured by a mortar shell and sent home. He was only eighteen years old.

Hemingway's life was an adventurous one in which he challenged nature and the dangers of war. He fought in the Spanish Civil War, was a correspondent in World War II, and ran with the bulls in Pamplona. He was an amateur boxer, avid hunter, and record-holding deep-sea fisherman.

Chapter 1 A Day's Wait 5

LITERARY TERM

Important literary terms are presented, preparing students to read fiction beyond the classroom.

IDIOMS AND EXPRESSIONS

A special focus on the meanings of idioms and expressions prepares students for authentic literature.

pride in his people (then referred to as Negroes) are evident in all of Hughes's writing.

At nineteen, Langston enrolled at Columbia University but left after a year. He traveled throughout Europe and Africa and worked at many jobs, including being a deckhand on a ship and a dishwasher in a Parisian nightclub. Money was always a problem, but he persevered and remained optimistic. Whether he was struggling as a student at Columbia University or working as a waiter in Washington, D.C., he continued writing poetry that praised his race for its beauty and humanity.

In the 1960s, Hughes chronicled the civil rights movement in the United States. He wrote about the sit-ins, the marches, the church bombings, the hatred, and the hope. His poem "I Dream a World" begins:

I dream a world where man
No other man will scorn
Where love will bless the earth
And peace its paths adorn.

Hughes died in 1967. His plays, poems, and stories are the legacy he left to the American people, who he hoped one day could live in racial harmony.

Thank You, Ma'm

She was a large woman with a large purse that had everything in it but a hammer and nails. It had a long strap, and she carried it slung across her shoulder. It was about eleven o'clock at night, dark, and she was walking alone, when a boy ran up behind her and tried to snatch her purse. The strap broke with the sudden single tug the boy gave it from behind. But the boy's weight and the weight of the purse combined caused him to lose his balance. Instead of taking off full blast as he had hoped, the boy fell on his back on the sidewalk and his legs flew up. The large woman simply turned around and kicked him right square in his blue-jeaned sitter. Then she reached down, picked the boy up by his shirt front, and shook him until his teeth rattled.

After that the woman said, "Pick up my pocketbook, boy, and give it here."

Chapter 2 Thank You, Ma'm

C UNDERSTANDING THE STORY

1 Reading Comprehension

Answer these questions to determine how well you understood the story:

1 The story is set in New York's Greenwich Village, at one time famous for its art colony. How do we know that the author is familiar with his setting?
2 Why does Johnsy feel she is fated to die?
3 Describe Mr. Behrman.
4 What was Mr. Behrman's masterpiece?
5 At what point in the story do you begin to think that Mr. Behrman will help Johnsy?
6 What was the ending of "The Last Leaf"? How did you feel when you reached the end of the story?

2 Guessing Meaning from Context

Read each of the following sentences. The words in **bold** are in the story. Find the words in the story and try to understand their meanings. Write a synonym for each word in the space provided at the end of the sentence.

1 The hiker had to **traverse** many paths before he found a stream to wash his face and hands. _walk across_

2 That **quaint** little house is a contrast to all the modern buildings surrounding it. _____

3 Cats often **prowl** all night, looking for food. _____

4 When we go to a party, we expect to meet **congenial** people.

_____

5 Frankenstein's monster was a **ravager** who roamed the countryside, causing widespread damage. _____

6 An epidemic often **smites** children and old people. _____

7 In medieval times, knights were expected to be **chivalric**.

_____

Chapter 4 The Last Leaf **63**

2 In 1849, when miners found gold in Alaska, they immediately staked a **claim**. _____

3 When I fell down, I got a **bump** on my head. _____

4 Maria is always **angling** to get special favors. _____

5 A good reporter must never **slant** the news. _____

6 After his sickness, his face had a **hollow** look. _____

7 Our **flight** to North Carolina was a short one. _____

8 The bullet just **glanced** off the policeman's shoulder. It didn't hurt him.

_____

9 I must pay the **premium** on my insurance policy. _____

3 Grammar: Reflexive and Intensive Pronouns

> In Jack Finney's story, the main character, Charley, discovers the third level by *himself*. What kind of pronoun is *himself*? It is called a reflexive pronoun because the word reflects back to the subject. For example, if you fell down and hurt your knee, you would say, "I hurt myself." Or, if you were trying to control a mischievous child, you might command, "Behave yourself."
>
> Like other personal pronouns, the *self* words have both singular and plural forms. The singular pronouns are: *myself, yourself, himself, herself, oneself,* and *itself*.
>
> You may also use a *self* pronoun for emphasis. These pronouns are called intensive pronouns, and they are written exactly the same as the reflexive pronouns. If Charley's wife didn't believe his story about the third level, he would insist, "I myself saw it." Note that this *self* pronoun immediately follows the subject.
>
> *Examples:*
> You yourself invited them.
> He himself made the call.
>
> *continued*

GRAMMAR

Students improve their reading comprehension by reviewing a grammar point modeled in the story.

2 Making Inferences

> Authors often write something that is intended to have more than one meaning. While you read, look for meanings that are not explicitly stated – these are inferences. Making inferences will help you enjoy the reading on a different level. The story now has deeper significance, and you will have a better understanding of it.

Read the following lines from the story. What can you infer about character, setting, plot, or theme? Write your answer on the line below.

1 He lay still in the bed and seemed very detached from what was going on. (lines 28–29)

Something was disturbing the boy. _____

2 "You don't have to stay in here with me, Papa, if it bothers you." (lines 41–42)

_____

3 At the house they said the boy had refused to let anyone come into the room. (lines 66–67)

_____

4 He was evidently holding tight onto himself about something. (lines 82–83)

_____

5 . . . and he cried very easily at little things that were of no importance. (lines 107–108)

_____

MAKING INFERENCES

Students practice making inferences, an important critical thinking skill in every academic discipline.

3 Analyzing the Story: Point of View

Look back at the Literary Term on page 5. The story is told from the father's point of view. The father observes Schatz and comes to a conclusion about his son's health. We, as readers, learn about Schatz from his father's observations.

On the lines below, write the father's observations about Schatz.

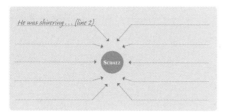

Pair Discussion   With a partner, compare what you have written. Correct any mistakes you find. How does Schatz change at the end of the story?

4 Writing

Read the writing ideas that follow. Your instructor may make specific assignments or ask you to choose one of these:

1 Pretend you are Schatz. Write a paragraph about what is going on in your mind as you lie in bed thinking about your illness. Use the present tense.
2 Describe a fear of death you may have had as a child. Were you ever injured or in a hospital when you were young?
3 How did you feel after reading the story? How did you relate to the boy and the father? Write about these feelings.
4 Create a conversation between the father and the doctor the next day.
5 Compare the characters of Schatz and his father.
6 Rewrite the story from the doctor's point of view.

16   A Life Lesson

ANALYZING THE STORY

Students refine their understanding of the literary term in a close reading of the story facilitated by a graphic organizer.

WRITING

A variety of writing assignments mirror response writing students will encounter in college.

---

20 She grabbed him on the neck and dragged him in the street.

_____

21 We worked hard to the summer.

_____

22 Students like to read stories about a adventurous heroes.

_____

23 Anna well played the trumpet.

_____

24 Panchito was impressed on what his teacher told him.

_____

25 The story "The Circuit" is set at the United States.

_____

WEBQUEST

Find more information about the topics in Part One by going on the Internet. Go to www.cambridge.org/discoveringfiction/wq and follow the instructions for doing a WebQuest. Have fun. Enjoy the quest!

WEBQUEST

Engaging WebQuests send students to authentic websites, building their confidence, fluency, and ability to read across different media.

Discovering Fiction

A READER OF NORTH AMERICAN SHORT STORIES

2

A Life Lesson

WE LEARN in different ways. When we think of learning, we usually think of teachers and school. However, a great deal of our learning takes place outside the classroom. Life is the greatest teacher of all, and our experiences often change our lives forever.

In the following stories, the main characters undergo important changes through a single incident or a chance meeting, as occurs in "Thank You, Ma'm." As you finish each story in this part, ask yourself, How did the characters learn a lesson? Have I ever experienced a similar situation? You might be surprised to find that you have learned a lesson just from reading these stories.

there were dark areas under his eyes. He lay still in the bed and seemed very detached from what was going on.

I read aloud from Howard Pyle's *Book of Pirates*; but I could see he was not following what I was reading.

"How do you feel, Schatz?" I asked him.

"Just the same, so far," he said.

I sat at the foot of the bed and read to myself while I waited for it to be time to give another capsule. It would have been natural for him to go to sleep, but when I looked up he was looking at the foot of the bed, looking very strangely.

"Why don't you try to go to sleep?

I'll wake you up for the medicine."

"I'd rather stay awake."

After a while he said to me, "You don't have to stay in here with me, Papa, if it bothers you."

"It doesn't bother me."

"No, I mean you don't have to stay if it's going to bother you."

I thought perhaps he was a little lightheaded and after giving him the prescribed capsules at eleven o'clock I went out for a while.

It was a bright, cold day, the ground covered with a sleet that had frozen so that it seemed as if all the bare trees, the bushes, the cut brush and all the grass and the bare ground had been varnished with ice. I took the young Irish setter for a little walk up the road and along a frozen creek, but it was difficult to stand or walk on the glassy surface and the red dog slipped and slithered and I fell twice, hard, once dropping my gun and having it slide away over the ice.

"... what time do you think I'm going to die?" he asked.

We flushed a covey of quail under a high clay bank with overhanging brush and I killed two as they went out of sight over the top of the bank. Some of the covey lit in trees, but most of them scattered into brush piles and it was necessary to jump on the ice-coated mounds of brush several times before they would flush. Coming out while you were poised unsteadily on the icy, springy brush they made difficult shooting and I killed two, missed five, and started back pleased to have found a covey close to the house and happy there were so many left to find another day.

At the house they said the boy had refused to let anyone come into the room.

"You can't come in," he said. "You mustn't get what I have."

I went up to him and found him in exactly the position I had left him, white-faced, but with the tops of his cheeks flushed by the fever, staring still, as he stared, at the foot of the bed.

I took his temperature.

"What is it?"

"Something like a hundred," I said. It was one hundred and two and
four tenths.

"It was a hundred and two," he said.

"Who said so?"

"The doctor."

"Your temperature is all right," I said. "It's nothing to worry about."

"I don't worry," he said, "but I can't keep from thinking."

"Don't think," I said. "Just take it easy."

"I'm taking it easy," he said and looked straight ahead. He was
evidently holding tight onto himself about something.

"Take this with water."

"Do you think it will do any good?"

"Of course it will."

I sat down and opened the Pirate book and commenced to read, but I
could see he was not following, so I stopped.

"About what time do you think I'm going to die?" he asked.

"What?"

"About how long will it be before I die?"

"You aren't going to die. What's the matter with you?"

"Oh, yes, I am. I heard him say a hundred and two."

"People don't die with a fever of one hundred and two. That's a silly
way to talk."

"I know they do. At school in France the boys told me you can't live
with forty-four degrees. I've got a hundred and two."

He had been waiting to die all day, ever since nine o'clock in the morning.

"You poor Schatz," I said. "Poor old Schatz. It's like miles and
kilometers. You aren't going to die. That's a different thermometer. On
that thermometer thirty-seven is normal. On this kind it's ninety-eight."

"Are you sure?"

"Absolutely," I said. "It's like miles and kilometers. You know, like
how many kilometers we make when we do seventy miles in the car?"

"Oh," he said.

But his gaze at the foot of the bed relaxed slowly. The hold over
himself relaxed too, finally, and the next day it was very slack and he
cried very easily at little things that were of no importance.

C UNDERSTANDING THE STORY

1 Reading Comprehension

Answer these questions to determine how well you understood the story:

1 In what season does the story take place?
2 How does the father know his son is sick?
3 Why doesn't the boy pay attention to the book his father is reading to him?
4 Where does the father go while his son is resting in bed?
5 What is the boy waiting for?
6 How much time passes from the beginning of the story until the end?
7 Why does the boy cry easily the next day?

2 Guessing Meaning from Context

The words in the list are in the story. Find the words in the story and try to understand their meanings. Write the appropriate word(s) in each sentence. Use each word only once.

flushed	detached	quail	varnished
capsule	lightheaded	poised	shivering
covey	sleet	bank	
commenced	pirates	prescribed	

1 The man, drenched by the rain, stood ___*shivering*___ in his wet clothes.

2 The little boy was too worried about his temperature to listen to stories of _____ and hidden treasure.

3 She felt _____ from the hot weather and lack of water.

4 Schatz's doctor _____ the medicine in _____ form.

5 The weather forecaster predicted a winter storm with snow and

_____ .

6 They _____ the antique furniture to protect it.

7 A _____ of _____ sat hidden in the bushes.

8 The hunter _____ his prey out of the woods.

9 The diver stood _____ at the edge of the diving board.

10 She sat apart from the other students feeling _____ and lonely.

11 At the signal from the instructor, the students _____ to take the exam.

12 An old gnarled tree stood on the _____ of the river.

3 Grammar: Articles and Prepositions

The small connecting words in English often present problems in our reading and writing. If you pay attention and practice using articles and prepositions, your writing will be more polished, and your spoken English will improve as well.

The English articles include *a*, *an*, and *the*. *The* is the definite article; it is used with nouns that refer to something or someone definite or specific. *A* and *an* are indefinite articles; they are used with nouns that refer to something or someone that is not specific or known about.

The indefinite articles *a* and *an* are used with singular nouns only. The definite article *the* can be used with a singular or plural noun.

Sometimes, singular nouns sound plural, for example, *news*, *family*, *orchestra*, and *army*. It is important to remember that such nouns still take a singular verb so that subject and verb agree.

Examples:
The **news** of his rescue is a relief.
The **family** next door **is coming** for dinner.
The **orchestra rehearses** every day.
An **army needs** equipment.

● Intangible or abstract nouns Nouns such as *love, life, hope, beauty,* and *hate* do not use any article when they are referred to in a general sense.

Example:
INCORRECT: The life is unpredictable.
CORRECT: **Life** is unpredictable.

● **Using articles** When we refer to a noun the first time, we use *a* or *an*. Thereafter, since the identity of the noun is established, we use the definite article *the*.

> *Example:*
> There is **a** large elm tree in the park. **The** tree is more than a hundred years old.

Prepositions, which occur frequently in English, act as bridges or connections between their objects and other words in a sentence. A preposition always has an object – a noun or pronoun. The preposition plus its object is called a prepositional phrase. Prepositional phrases may occur anywhere in a sentence. At the beginning of a sentence, the prepositional phrase is usually followed by a comma. Here are some examples of prepositional phrases:

> The story **of her recovery** is an inspiration.
> We saw the clouds **above the mountain**.
> **After the summer**, we will visit France.

● **Using prepositions** The following are some frequently used prepositions:

about	from	over	without
above	below	in	through
after	by	into	to
among	down	of	under
around	during	off	up
at	for	on	with

The prepositions *in* and *on* are often confused. When we are discussing time, *on* refers to a specific date.

> *Examples:*
> I was born **on** April 5, 1950.
> I was born **in** April; or I was born **in** 1950.

Application 1   Write the correct articles in these sentences.

1 I read _____*the*_____ book *The Color Purple* before I saw _____*the*_____ movie.

2 The house has _____ beautiful garden. Would you like to sit in _____ garden?

3 _____ police found _____ kidnapped child.

4 He bought _____ expensive car, and he washes _____ car every week.

5 _____ bank was closed because it was _____ holiday.

6 I didn't have _____ stamp, so I couldn't mail _____ letter.

7 She asked _____ waiter to bring her _____ menu.

8 Did you submit _____ application for _____ credit card?

Application 2   Write the correct prepositions in the sentences below. For some sentences, there is more than one correct preposition.

1 The man _____*in*_____ the car looked suspicious.

2 He gave some money _____ the beggar.

3 _____ the meeting, we went _____ the cafeteria _____ lunch.

4 As he stepped _____ the street, he heard the screeching sound _____ brakes.

5 He was heartbroken _____ her betrayal, but he hoped he would fall _____ love again.

6 They jogged _____ the park _____ the rain.

7 We celebrate Independence Day _____ July 4.

8 Are you taking a trip _____ January?

Often, a preposition consists of a group of words. The following are typical examples:

in front of	because of	by means of	according to
next to	in place of	in order to	in spite of

Application 3   Use the preceding prepositions (groups of words) in the following sentences.

1 We played the game ___*according to*___ the rules.

2 _____ his disability, he graduated with honors.

3 He used chopsticks _____ a fork.

4 It was hard to see the stage because the man _____ me wore a hat.

5 He turned up the volume _____ hear the music better.

6 _____ a hidden camera, the police were able to trap the terrorist.

7 _____ the blizzard, travelers were stranded at the airport.

8 He enjoyed sitting _____ the window and watching the children play.

Note: The omission of prepositions is a common error. If you read your sentences aloud, often you will hear the mistake and correct it yourself. Trust your ear for the language!

Application 4   For this exercise you need to combine the various things you have just learned. Use appropriate articles and prepositions to complete the following sentences.

1 He came ___*into*___ ___*the*___ room to shut ___*the*___ windows while we were still in bed.

2 When I put my hand _____ his forehead, I knew he had

_____ fever.

3 Downstairs, _____ doctor left three different medicines _____

different colored capsules _____ instructions _____ giving

them.

4 Back _____ _____ room, I wrote _____ boy's

temperature down and made _____ note _____ _____

time to give _____ various capsules.

5 It was _____ bright, cold day, _____ ground covered

_____ sleet.

6 I took _____ young Irish setter _____ _____ little walk

_____ _____ road.

7 People don't die _____ _____ fever _____ one hundred

and two.

8 _____ school _____ France, _____ boys told me you

can't live _____ forty-four degrees.

D THINKING CRITICALLY

1 Discussing the Story

Discuss the following questions with a partner, in a small group, or with the whole class:

1 Describe the relationship between the boy and his father. Are they close? How do they communicate? Is there a mother in this family? Where is she?
2 Why doesn't Schatz tell his father that he is afraid?
3 How does the father sense Schatz's fear?
4 How does Hemingway portray the boy and the father?
5 Choose another title for the story.

2 Making Inferences

Authors often write something that is intended to have more than
one meaning. While you read, look for meanings that are not
explicitly stated – these are inferences. Making inferences will help
you enjoy the reading on a different level. The story now has deeper
significance, and you will have a better understanding of it.

Read the following lines from the story. What can you infer about
character, setting, plot, or theme? Write your answer on the line below.

1 He lay still in the bed and seemed very detached from what was going on.
(lines 28–29)

Something was disturbing the boy.

2 "You don't have to stay in here with me, Papa, if it bothers you."
(lines 41–42)

3 At the house they said the boy had refused to let anyone come into the
room. (lines 66–67)

4 He was evidently holding tight onto himself about something. (lines 82–83)

5 . . . and he cried very easily at little things that were of no importance.
(lines 107–108)

3 Analyzing the Story: Point of View

Look back at the Literary Term on page 5. The story is told from the father's point of view. The father observes Schatz and comes to a conclusion about his son's health. We, as readers, learn about Schatz from his father's observations.

On the lines below, write the father's observations about Schatz.

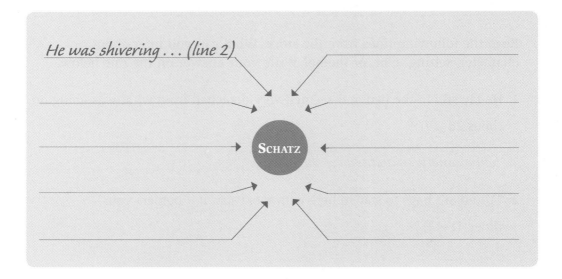

He was shivering . . . (line 2)

Pair Discussion   With a partner, compare what you have written. Correct any mistakes you find. How does Schatz change at the end of the story?

4 Writing

Read the writing ideas that follow. Your instructor may make specific assignments or ask you to choose one of these:

1 Pretend you are Schatz. Write a paragraph about what is going on in your mind as you lie in bed thinking about your illness. Use the present tense.
2 Describe a fear of death you may have had as a child. Were you ever injured or in a hospital when you were young?
3 How did you feel after reading the story? How did you relate to the boy and the father? Write about these feelings.
4 Create a conversation between the father and the doctor the next day.
5 Compare the characters of Schatz and his father.
6 Rewrite the story from the doctor's point of view.

CHAPTER 2

Thank You, Ma'm

LANGSTON HUGHES

A PREPARING TO READ

1 Think Before You Read

Read the first paragraph of the story once and think of it as describing the opening scene of a play. Then answer the following questions:

1 Who are the characters in this scene?
2 What is happening?
3 Where and when is the action taking place?
4 Why does the action take place?
5 Do you think a chance encounter between people can sometimes change their lives? Think about chance or fate as you read this story.

2 Literary Term: Dialect

A **dialect** consists of words or phrases that reflect the regional variety of a language. An author or playwright will often use a regional dialect to make the dialogue more authentic. Initially, a dialect may be difficult to understand; it is similar to watching a foreign film with subtitles. However, the language will become more comfortable as you continue reading, and the rhythm of the dialect will be as natural as if you were one of the characters.

The following examples of dialect occur in the story:

ain't	aren't	**I didn't aim to**	I didn't intend to
gonna	going to	**sit you down**	sit down
could of	could have	**I were**	I was
late as it be	late as it is	**fix us**	prepare for us

3 Idioms and Expressions

You will find these idioms and expressions in the story:

I got a great mind to I should	**took care** was careful
get through with finish	**set the table** put out plates, glasses, and so forth
make a dash for it run away	

B THE STORY

About the Author

Langston Hughes (1902–1967) had a varied career that took him far away from his birthplace in Joplin, Missouri. His early love for reading books was encouraged by his mother, who often took him to the library. His mother also wrote poetry and gave dramatic readings. Her work required her to travel extensively.

After his parents separated, his father moved to Mexico and Hughes went to live with his maternal grandmother. She, too, had an influence on his future career. She was a good storyteller, and she often told him about the days of slavery. The maternal influence and the sense of deep pride in his people (then referred to as Negroes) are evident in all of Hughes's writing.

At nineteen, Langston enrolled at Columbia University but left after a year. He traveled throughout Europe and Africa and worked at many jobs, including being a deckhand on a ship and a dishwasher in a Parisian nightclub. Money was always a problem, but he persevered and remained optimistic. Whether he was struggling as a student at Columbia University or working as a waiter in Washington, D.C., he continued writing poetry that praised his race for its beauty and humanity.

In the 1960s, Hughes chronicled the civil rights movement in the United States. He wrote about the sit-ins, the marches, the church bombings, the hatred, and the hope. His poem "I Dream a World" begins:

I dream a world where man

No other man will scorn

Where love will bless the earth

And peace its paths adorn.

Hughes died in 1967. His plays, poems, and stories are the legacy he left to the American people, who he hoped one day could live in racial harmony.

Thank You, Ma'm

She was a large woman with a large purse that had everything in it but a hammer and nails. It had a long strap, and she carried it slung across her shoulder. It was about eleven o'clock at night, dark, and she was walking alone, when a boy ran up behind her and tried to snatch
5 her purse. The strap broke with the sudden single tug the boy gave it from behind. But the boy's weight and the weight of the purse combined caused him to lose his balance. Instead of taking off full blast as he had hoped, the boy fell on his back on the sidewalk and his legs flew up. The large woman simply turned around and kicked him right square in
10 his blue-jeaned sitter. Then she reached down, picked the boy up by his shirt front, and shook him until his teeth rattled.

After that the woman said, "Pick up my pocketbook, boy, and give it here."

She still held him tightly. But she bent down enough to permit him
to stoop and pick up her purse. Then she said, "Now ain't you ashamed
of yourself?"

Firmly gripped by his shirt front, the boy said, "Yes'm."

The woman said, "What did you want to do it for?"

The boy said, "I didn't aim to."

By that time two or three people passed, stopped, turned to look, and
some stood watching.

"If I turn you loose, will you run?" asked the woman.

"Yes'm," said the boy.

"Then I won't turn you loose," said the woman. She did not release him.

"Lady, I'm sorry," whispered the boy.

"Um-hum! Your face is dirty. I got a great mind to wash your face for
you. Ain't you got nobody home to tell you to wash your face?"

"No'm," said the boy.

"Then it will get washed this evening," said the large woman, starting
up the street, dragging the frightened boy behind her.

He looked as if he were fourteen or fifteen, frail and willow-wild in
tennis shoes and blue jeans.

The woman said, "You ought to be my son. I would teach you right from
wrong. Least I can do right now is to wash your face. Are you hungry?"

"No'm," said the being-dragged boy. "I just want you to turn me loose."

"Was I bothering you when I turned that corner?" asked the woman.

"No'm."

"But you put yourself in contact with me," said the woman. "If you
think that contact is not going to last awhile, you got another thought
coming. When I get through with you, sir, you are going to remember
Mrs. Luella Bates Washington Jones."

Sweat popped out on the boy's face and he began to struggle. Mrs.
Jones stopped, jerked him around in front of her, put a half-nelson
about his neck, and continued to drag him up the street. When she got
to her door, she dragged the boy inside, down a hall, and into a large
kitchenette-furnished room at the rear of the house. She switched on the
light and left the door open. The boy could hear other roomers laughing
and talking in the large house. Some of their doors were open, too, so he
knew he and the woman were not alone. The woman still had him by
the neck in the middle of her room.

She said, "What is your name?"

"Roger," answered the boy.

"Then, Roger, you go to that sink and wash your face," said the
woman, whereupon she turned him loose – at last. Roger looked at the
door – looked at the woman – looked at the door – and went to the sink.

"Let the water run until it gets warm," she said. "Here's a clean towel."

"You gonna take me to jail?" asked the boy, bending over the sink.

"Not with that face, I would not take you nowhere," said the woman. "Here I am trying to get home to cook me a bite to eat, and you snatch my pocketbook! Maybe you ain't been to your supper either, late as it be. Have you?"

"There's nobody home at my house," said the boy.

"Then we'll eat," said the woman. "I believe you're hungry – or been hungry – to try to snatch my pocketbook!"

"I want a pair of blue suede shoes," said the boy.

"Well, you didn't have to snatch my pocketbook to get some suede shoes," said Mrs. Luella Bates Washington Jones. "You could of asked me."

"Ma'm?"

The water dripping from his face, the boy looked at her. There was a long pause. A very long pause. After he had dried his face and not knowing what else to do, dried it again, the boy turned around, wondering what next. The door was open. He would make a dash for it down the hall. He would run, run, run!

The woman was sitting on the day bed. After a while, she said, "I were young once and I wanted things I could not get."

There was another long pause. The boy's mouth opened. Then he frowned, not knowing he frowned.

The woman said, "Um-hum! You thought I was going to say but, didn't you? You thought I was going to say, but I didn't snatch people's pocketbooks. Well, I wasn't going to say that." Pause. Silence. "I have done things, too, which I would not tell you, son – neither tell God, if He didn't already know. Everybody's got something in common. Sit you down while I fix us something to eat. You might run that comb through your hair so you will look presentable."

In another corner of the room behind a screen was a gas plate and an icebox. Mrs. Jones got up and went behind the screen. The woman did not watch the boy to see if he was going to run now, nor did she watch her purse, which she left behind her on the day bed. But the boy took care to sit on the far side of the room, away from the purse, where he thought she could easily see him out of the corner of her eye if she wanted to. He did not trust the woman to trust him. And he did not trust the woman not to trust him. And he did not want to be mistrusted now.

"Do you need somebody to go to the store," asked the boy, "maybe to get some milk or something?"

"Don't believe I do," said the woman, "unless you just want sweet milk yourself. I was going to make cocoa out of this canned milk I got here."

She heated some lima beans and ham she had in the icebox, made the cocoa, and set the table. The woman did not ask the boy anything about where he lived, or his folks, or anything else that would embarrass him. Instead, as they ate, she told him about her job in a hotel beauty shop that stayed open late, what the work was like, and how all kinds of

women came in and out, blondes, redheads and Spanish. Then she cut
him half of her ten-cent cake.

"Eat some more, son," she said.

105   When they finished eating, she got up and said, "Now here, take this
ten dollars and buy yourself some blue suede shoes. And, next time, do
not make the mistake of latching onto my pocketbook nor nobody else's
– because shoes got by devilish ways will burn your feet. I got to get my
rest now. But from here on in, son, I hope you will behave yourself."

110   She led the way down the hall to the front door and opened it. "Good
night! Behave yourself, boy!" she said, looking into the street as he went
down the steps.

The boy wanted to say something other than "Thank you, ma'm,"
to Mrs. Luella Bates Washington Jones, but although his lips moved, he
115   couldn't even say that, as he turned at the foot of the barren stoop and
looked up at the large woman in the door. Then she shut the door.

C UNDERSTANDING THE STORY

1 Reading Comprehension

Answer these questions to determine how well you understood the story:

1 How old do you think Mrs. Jones is? –) 50 to 60
2 How does she feel about Roger? Is she angry at him? Does she like him?
3 At what point in the story does Mrs. Jones show that she cares about Roger?
4 Describe Roger's physical appearance. →thin, weedy
5 Describe his behavior. →child, emborres, quiet
6 How does Mrs. Jones treat Roger initially? How does her behavior change?
7 Find examples of sentences that show Mrs. Jones understands Roger
very well.

She was angry
oath, after sharestic

2 Guessing Meaning from Context

The words below are in the story. Find the words in the story and try to
understand their meanings. Look at the four definitions for each word and
circle the correct one.

1 tug
   a force   c pull
   b steal   d shoot

2 permit
   a allow   c keep
   b push   d worry

3 stoop
   a forget   **c** run away
   b bend over   **d** fool

4 frail
   a strong   **c** tall
   b athletic   **d** delicate

5 bothering
   a whispering   **c** annoying
   b stealing   **d** meeting

6 sweat
   a perspiration   **c** cake
   b dessert   **d** blasphemy

7 snatch
   a trick   **c** watch
   b grab   **d** follow

8 frowned
   a grimaced   **c** discovered
   b smiled   **d** laughed

3 Grammar: Verb Tenses and Irregular Forms

Tenses indicate time. In English, we use six tenses – three simple and three perfect. The simple tenses are past, present, and future. The perfect tenses are past perfect, present perfect, and future perfect.

● Simple tenses The simple tenses are more specific about when an action or state of being occurs.

Examples:
PAST: They **ran** in the marathon.
PRESENT: They **run** in the marathon every year.
FUTURE: They **will run** in the marathon next year.

● Perfect tenses The perfect tenses show the time an action or state of being begins and is completed (perfected).

continued

In the present perfect tense, a situation exists up to now (the present). The construction would be: *has* (third person singular) or *have* + the past participle.

Examples:
He **has run** in five previous marathons. (up to now)
They **have run** in many marathons. (up to the present time)

In the past perfect tense, the situation was completed by the time another past event occurred. The past perfect can be thought of as a previous past. When a sentence describes two past events, the past perfect tense indicates what happened first. The construction would be: *had* + the past participle.

Example:
He **had run** in several marathons before he finished in first place.

The future perfect tense describes an action or state of being that we are predicting for a time in the future. The construction would be: *will have* + the past participle.

Example:
By next year, they **will have run** in ten marathons.

● Using the present perfect with *for* and *since* When you use *since* and *for* to indicate that a passage of time has elapsed, use the perfect tenses. Remember: Use *since* when you mention an exact date (day, month, or year), and use *for* when you show a period of time.

Examples:
He **has lived** in Hong Kong since 1997. (exact year)
He **has lived** in Hong Kong for ten years. (He still lives in
   Hong Kong.)

Most verbs in English change to the past tense by adding -*ed* or -*d* (if the verb already ends in an *e*). However, there are more than one hundred irregular verbs, and these verbs do not follow this rule. The simple past and past participle forms of irregular verbs are listed in the Appendix on pages 264–266.

Application 1   Write the correct present perfect verb form in the following sentences.

1 We ___*have studied*___ (study) for the exam for a week.

2 Since last week, he _____ (write) five pages of his novel.

3 She _____ (fall) many times since she started rollerblading.

4 For many weeks, the jury _____ (hear) testimony.

5 Since last year, Carl _____ (feel) happy at work.

6 Michelle _____ (sleep) late since she was a teenager.

Application 2   Some of the most troublesome irregular verbs are dealt with in the exercise that follows. For each sentence, write the verb(s) in the simple past or one of the perfect tenses. Read the sentences aloud.

1 It ___*had begun*___ (begin) to rain before we arrived at the stadium.

2 The children _____ (begin) to sing a song after the teacher _____ (begin) playing the piano.

3 He _____ (bear) the burden of supporting his family for many years.

4 The wild dog _____ (bite) the hunter. It was the first time the dog _____ (bite) anyone.

5 He _____ (buy) a corsage for his girlfriend. It was the first time he _____ (buy) her flowers.

6 The voters _____ (choose) a new president on Election Day.

7 The morning dew _____ (cling) to the rose petals.

8 The two lions _____ (creep) slowly toward their prey.

9 As they watched the sunset, they _____ (drink) their tea and _____ (dream) of former days.

10 After the apples _____ (fall) from the trees, we _____ (find) them on the ground.

11 Her grandfather _____ (teach) her many things before she _____ (leave) for college.

12 The lake _____ (freeze) two weeks ago, and we _____ (slide) on it as we walked.

13 She was pleased to see that her nephew _____ (grow) into a fine adult.

14 We _____ (hear) the loud music blasting from their car stereo.

15 The scout _____ (lead) the way through the woods. He _____ (be) their guide many times before.

16 The thief _____ (hide) the jewels, and the police never found out where he _____ (put) them.

Application 3   These sentences are taken from Hughes's story. Fill in the past tense forms of the verbs in parentheses.

1 The strap ____*broke*____ (break) with the sudden, single tug.

2 The boy _____ (fall) on his back, and his legs _____ (fly) up.

3 She _____ (shake) him until his teeth rattled.

4 She still _____ (hold) him tightly.

5 Then she _____ (say), "Now ain't you ashamed of yourself?"

6 He _____ (begin) to struggle.

7 He _____ (think) she could easily see him.

8 As they _____ (eat), she told him about her job.

9 All kinds of women _____ (come) into the beauty shop.

10 She _____ (cut) him half of her ten-cent cake.

11 When they finished eating, she _____ (stand) up.

12 She _____ (lead) the way down the hall.

Application 4 The past participle form of a verb may be used as an adjective. In sentences 4, 6, 10, 13, and 16 of Application 2 on pages 25 and 26, change the first verb in parentheses into the past participle form and combine it with the noun it modifies. For example,

the **frozen** lake
the **stolen** money

4 Editing

Edit the following essay. Correct any errors in grammar, spelling, or punctuation.

I think mrs Jones teached the boy a good lesson she could of reported him to Police but instead she decided she would taught him a lesson herself. The boy who was lucky she was a good-hearted person done wrong when he stealed her purse. I bet he didn't espect this old lady to be strong enuf to knock him over and drag him to her house and he was afraid to run away and also he liked her. She cared more for him then his own family. The boy was lucky to meet someone like mrs jones.

D THINKING CRITICALLY

1 Discussing the Story

Discuss the following questions with a partner, in a small group, or with the whole class:

1 How does Mrs. Jones react when Roger tries to steal her purse?
2 Is her reaction believable? Why or why not?
3 When they arrive at the boarding house, what do you think Roger is thinking or planning to do?
4 Does Mrs. Jones like the boy? Why?
5 How do you think Roger's encounter with Mrs. Jones alters his life?
6 Why does Hughes title the story, "Thank You, Ma'm"?

2 Making Inferences

> Authors often write something that is intended to have more than one meaning. While you read, look for meanings that are not explicitly stated – these are inferences. Making inferences will help you enjoy the reading on a different level. The story now has deeper significance, and you will have a better understanding of it.

Read the following lines from the story. What can you infer about character, setting, plot, or theme? Write your answer on the line below.

1 "When I get through with you, sir, you are going to remember Mrs. Luella Bates Washington Jones." (lines 40–41)

You will learn a lesson from me.

2 She switched on the light and left the door open. (lines 46–47)

3 "I were young once and I wanted things I could not get." (lines 74–75)

4 "I have done things, too, which I would not tell you. . . ." (lines 80–81)

5 . . . shoes got by devilish ways will burn your feet. (line 108)

3 Analyzing the Story: Dialect

Look back at the Literary Term on page 18. The woman and the boy use many examples of dialect. Read the meanings on the left. For each line, find a line in the story that has an equivalent meaning. An example has been done for you.

MEANING	LINES FROM THE STORY
1 Don't you have someone at home who tells you to wash your face?	*Ain't you got nobody home to tell you to wash your face? (line 27)*
2 Why did you try to steal my purse?	
3 I didn't plan to steal it.	
4 I should wash your face.	
5 I was young once.	
6 I'll cook dinner. I'll prepare dinner.	

Pair Discussion   With a partner, compare what you have written. Correct any mistakes you find. Can you think of some examples of dialect used in your local area?

4 Writing

Read the writing ideas that follow. Your instructor may make specific assignments or ask you to choose one of these:

1 Continue the story, assuming that the characters meet again. Write a dialogue between Roger and Mrs. Jones. Describe their second encounter – a week later, a month later, or a year later.
2 Describe Mrs. Jones and the way she treats Roger. Describe Roger and the way he responds to Mrs. Jones.
3 Write a different ending to the story. For example, Mrs. Jones calls the police, or Roger runs away.
4 Have you ever had a purse or wallet stolen from you? How did you feel? Write about the experience.
5 Juvenile crime can be a problem in the United States. Compare the situation with that in your country.
6 Who should be responsible for the moral education of a child? Parents? Society? Schools? Write about your opinion and give reasons for it.

CHAPTER 3

The Circuit

Francisco Jimenez

A PREPARING TO READ

1 Think Before You Read

Answer the following questions before you read the story:

1 Have you ever moved with your family to a new place?
2 Describe how you felt. Were you excited about moving? Were you nervous about meeting new friends?
3 When parents move children around because of jobs, how do you think the children feel?
4 What do you know about migrant workers? What kind of work do migrant workers usually find?

2 Literary Term: Sense Impressions

Sometimes, words are so vivid that we can see, smell, or taste objects that the writer describes. We can hear the sounds, and see and feel things just as the character does. These descriptions are called **sense impressions**. For example, in the story you are about to read, the author describes the main protagonist as "soaked in sweat." Can you visualize what a person "soaked in sweat" looks and feels like? As you read the story, be aware of any other expressions that may appeal to one of your five senses.

3 Idioms and Expressions

You will find these idioms and expressions in the story:

in store for me what was going to happen (in this context, negative)	**turn pale** to be afraid
	taking roll taking attendance in class
picked up bought cheaply	**felt my blood rush to my head** a sudden feeling of intense anxiety
a lump in my throat a feeling of pressure in the throat caused by a strong emotional feeling of sadness and regret	
	gave me goose bumps raised spots on the skin caused by a strong feeling of excitement
eyes glued on to look at something intensely for a long time	

B THE STORY

About the Author

Francisco Jimenez (born 1943) moved with his family to the United States when he was four. Francisco soon began working in the fields in Southern California. Life as migrant workers was difficult for the Jimenez family. Francisco Jimenez would often start in a new school and leave the following week because the family had to follow the crops. Money was always a problem, especially as the family grew larger. However, Francisco wanted to complete his education.

Despite the odds, Jimenez followed his dream of getting an education, and he received a doctorate from Columbia University in New York City. Jimenez began teaching in 1971 and is now a professor at the University of Santa Clara in California.

"The Circuit" comes from a collection of stories based on the life of Panchito (the nickname for Francisco Jimenez). "The Circuit" was published in 1973 in the *Arizona Quarterly* and received the Best Short Fiction Award.

Francisco Jimenez is bilingual and bicultural and feels privileged to be able to write in both English and Spanish.

The Circuit

It was that time of year again. Ito, the strawberry share-cropper, did not smile. It was natural. The peak of the strawberry season was over, and the last few days the workers, most of them braceros,[1] were not picking as many boxes as they had during the months of June and July.

5   As the last days of August disappeared, so did the number of braceros. Sunday, only one – the best picker – came to work. I liked him. Sometimes we talked during our half-hour lunch break. That is how I found out he was from Jalisco, the same state in Mexico my family was from. That Sunday was the last time I saw him.

10   When the sun had tired and sunk behind the mountains, Ito signalled us that it was time to go home. "Ya esora,"[2] he yelled in his broken Spanish. Those were the words I waited for twelve hours a day, every day, seven days a week, week after week. And the thought of not hearing them again saddened me.

15   As we drove home, Papà did not say a word. With both hands on the wheel, he stared at the dirt road. My older brother, Roberto, was also silent. He leaned his head back and closed his eyes. Once in a while he cleared from his throat the dust that blew in from outside.

Yes, it was that time of year. When I opened the front door to the
20   shack, I stopped. Everything we owned was neatly packed in cardboard boxes. Suddenly I felt even more the weight of hours, days, weeks, and months of work. I sat down on a box. The thought of having to move

---

[1]**braceros**: laborers
[2]**Ya esora**: It's time

to Fresno and knowing what was in store for me there brought tears to my eyes.

That night before five o'clock in the morning, Papà woke everyone up. A few minutes later, the yelling and screaming of my little brothers and sisters, for whom the move was a great adventure, broke the silence of dawn. Shortly, the barking of the dogs accompanied them.

While we packed the breakfast dishes, Papà went outside to start the "Carcanchita." That was the name Papà gave his old '38 black Plymouth. He bought it in a used-car lot in Santa Rosa in the winter of 1949. Papà was very proud of his little jalopy.[3] He had a right to be proud of it. He spent a lot of time looking at other cars before buying this one. When he finally chose the Carcanchita, he checked it thoroughly before driving it out of the car lot. He examined every inch of the car. He listened to the motor, tilting his head from side to side like a parrot, trying to detect any noises that spelled car trouble. After being satisfied with the looks and sounds of the car, Papà then insisted on knowing who the original owner was. He never did find out from the car salesman, but he bought the car anyway. Papà figured the original owner must have been an important man, because behind the rear seat of the car he found a necktie.

Papà parked the car out in front and left the motor running. "Listo,"[4] he yelled. Without saying a word, Roberto and I began to carry the boxes out to the car. Roberto carried the two big boxes and I carried the two smaller ones. Papà then threw the mattress on top of the car roof and tied it with ropes to the front and rear bumpers.

Everything was packed except Mamà's pot. It was an old, large galvanized pot she had picked up at an army surplus store in Santa Maria the year I was born. The pot had many dents and nicks, and the more dents and nicks it acquired the more Mamà liked it. "Mi olla,"[5] she used to say proudly.

I held the front door open as Mamà carefully carried out her pot by both handles, making sure not to spill the cooked beans. When she got to the car, Papà reached out to help her with it. Roberto opened the rear car door and Papà gently placed it on the floor behind the front seat. All of us then climbed in. Papà sighed, wiped the sweat off his forehead with his sleeve, and said wearily: "Es todo."[6]

As we drove away, I felt a lump in my throat. I turned around and looked at our little shack for the last time.

At sunset we drove into a labor camp near Fresno. Since Papà did not speak English, Mamà asked the camp foreman if he needed any more

---

[3]**jalopy (carcanchita)**: a decrepit, old car
[4]**Listo**: Ready
[5]**Mi olla**: My pot
[6]**Es todo**: That's all

workers. "We don't need no more," said the foreman, scratching his
head. "Check with Sullivan down the road. Can't miss him. He lives in
65 a big white house with a fence around it."

When we got there, Mamà walked up to the house. She went through
a white gate, past a row of rosebushes, up the stairs to the front door.
She rang the doorbell. The porch light went on and a tall, husky man
came out. They exchanged a few words. After the man went in, Mamà
70 clasped her hands and hurried back to the car. "We have work! Mr.
Sullivan said we can stay there the whole season," she said, gasping
and pointing to an old garage near the stables.

The garage was worn out by the years. It had no windows. The walls,
eaten by termites, strained to support the roof, full of holes. The dirt
75 floor, populated by earthworms, looked like a gray road map.

That night, by the light of a kerosene lamp, we unpacked and cleaned
our new home. Roberto swept away the loose dirt, leaving the hard
ground. Papà plugged the holes in the walls with old newspapers and
tin can tops. Mamà fed my little brothers and sisters. Papà and Roberto
80 then brought in the mattress and placed it on the far corner of the
garage. "Mamà, you and the little ones sleep on the mattress. Roberto,
Panchito, and I will sleep outside under the trees," Papà said.

Early next morning Mr. Sullivan showed us where his crop was, and
after breakfast, Papà, Roberto, and I headed for the vineyard to pick.
85 Around nine o'clock the temperature had risen to almost one hundred
degrees. I was completely soaked in sweat and my mouth felt as if I had
been chewing on a handkerchief. I walked over to the end of the row,
picked up the jug of water we had brought, and began drinking. "Don't
drink too much; you'll get sick," Roberto shouted. No sooner had he said
90 that than I felt sick to my stomach. I dropped to my knees and let the jug
roll off my hands. I remained motionless with my eyes glued on the hot
sandy ground. All I could hear was the drone of insects. Slowly I began
to recover. I poured water over my face and neck and watched the dirty
water run down my arms to the ground.
95 I still felt a little dizzy when we took a break to eat lunch. It was
past two o'clock, and we sat underneath a large walnut tree that was
on the side of the road. While we ate, Papà jotted down the number
of boxes we had picked. Roberto drew designs on the ground with a
stick. Suddenly I noticed Papà's face turn pale as he looked down the
100 road. "Here comes the school bus," he whispered loudly in alarm.
Instinctively, Roberto and I ran and hid in the vineyards. We did not
want to get in trouble for not going to school. The neatly dressed boys
about my age got off. They carried books under their arms. After they
crossed the street, the bus drove away. Roberto and I came out from
105 hiding and joined Papà. "Tienen que tener cuidado,"[7] he warned us.

---

[7]**Tienen que tener cuidado**: You have to be careful

After lunch we went back to work. The sun kept beating down. The buzzing insects, the wet sweat, and the hot, dry dust made the afternoon seem to last forever. Finally the mountains around the valley reached out and swallowed the sun. Within an hour it was too dark to continue picking. The vines blanketed the grapes, making it difficult to see the bunches. "Vàmonos,"[8] said Papà, signalling to us that it was time to quit work. Papà then took out a pencil and began to figure out how much we had earned our first day. He wrote down numbers, crossed some out, wrote down some more. "Quince,"[9] he murmured.

When we arrived home, we took a cold shower underneath a water hose. We then sat down to eat dinner around some wooden crates that served as a table. Mamà had cooked a special meal for us. We had rice and tortillas with carne con chile, my favorite dish.

The next morning I could hardly move. My body ached all over. I felt little control over my arms and legs. This feeling went on every morning for days until my muscles finally got used to the work.

It was Monday, the first week of November. The grape season was over and I could now go to school. I woke up early that morning and lay in bed, looking at the stars and savoring the thought of not going to work and of starting sixth grade for the first time that year. Since I could not sleep, I decided to get up and join Papà and Roberto at breakfast. I sat at the table across from Roberto, but I kept my head down. I did not want to look up and face him. I knew he was sad. He was not going to school today. He was not going tomorrow, or next week, or next month. He would not go until the cotton season was over, and that was sometime in February. I rubbed my hands together and watched the dry, acid-stained skin fall to the floor in little rolls.

When Papà and Roberto left for work, I felt relief. I walked to the top of a small grade next to the shack and watched the Carcanchita disappear in the distance in a cloud of dust.

Two hours later, around eight o'clock, I stood by the side of the road waiting for school bus number twenty. When it arrived, I climbed in. Everyone was busy either talking or yelling. I sat in an empty seat in the back.

When the bus stopped in front of the school, I felt very nervous. I looked out the bus window and saw boys and girls carrying books under their arms. I put my hands in my pant pockets and walked to the principal's office. When I entered, I heard a woman's voice say: "May I help you?" I was startled. I had not heard English for months. For a few seconds I remained speechless. I looked at the lady, who waited for an answer. My first instinct was to answer her in Spanish, but I held back.

---

[8]**Vamonos**: Let's go
[9]**Quince**: Fifteen

Finally, after struggling for English words, I managed to tell her that I wanted to enroll in the sixth grade. After answering many questions, I was led to the classroom.

150 Mr. Lema, the sixth-grade teacher, greeted me and assigned me a desk. He then introduced me to the class. I was so nervous and scared at that moment when everyone's eyes were on me that I wished I were with Papà and Roberto picking cotton. After taking roll, Mr. Lema gave the class the assignment for the first hour. "The first thing we have to
155 do this morning is finish reading the story we began yesterday," he said enthusiastically. He walked up to me, handed me an English book, and asked me to read. "We are on page 125," he said politely. When I heard this, I felt my blood rush to my head; I felt dizzy. "Would you like to read?" he asked hesitantly. I opened the book to page 125. My mouth
160 was dry. My eyes began to water. I could not begin. "You can read later," Mr. Lema said understandingly.

For the rest of the reading period I kept getting angrier and angrier with myself. *I should have read*, I thought to myself.

During recess I went into the restroom and opened my English book
165 to page 125. I began to read in a low voice, pretending I was in class. There were many words I did not know. I closed the book and headed back to the classroom.

Mr. Lema was sitting at his desk correcting papers. When I entered he looked up at me and smiled. I felt better. I walked up to him and
170 asked if he could help me with the new words. "Gladly," he said.

The rest of the month I spent my lunch hours working on English with Mr. Lema, my best friend at school.

One Friday, during lunch hour, Mr. Lema asked me to take a walk with him to the music room. "Do you like music?" he asked me as we
175 entered the building.

"Yes, I like corridos,"[10] I answered. He then picked up a trumpet, blew on it, and handed it to me. The sound gave me goose bumps. I knew that sound. I had heard it in many corridos.[10] "How would you like to learn how to play it?" he asked. He must have read my face
180 because before I could answer, he added: "I'll teach you how to play it during our lunch hours."

That day I could hardly wait to get home to tell Papà and Mamà the great news. As I got off the bus, my little brothers and sisters ran up to meet me. They were yelling and screaming. I thought they were
185 happy to see me, but when I opened the door to our shack, I saw that everything we owned was neatly packed in cardboard boxes.

---

[10]**corridos**: a popular type of Mexican song which tells a story

C UNDERSTANDING THE STORY

1 Reading Comprehension

Answer these questions to determine how well you understood the story:

1 The first part of the story is set in summer. What does the family pick in each season? Which season is NOT mentioned in the story?
2 Who in the family speaks English? Who does NOT speak English?
3 Which sentences describe what happens to the narrator, Panchito, working in the vineyard on the first day?
4 Why do the brothers hide when the school bus comes?
5 How does Mr. Lema help Panchito feel more comfortable on the first day of school?
6 What does Panchito see when he comes home on his last day of school? What does Panchito understand as a result of this?

2 Guessing Meaning from Context

The words below are in the story. Find the words in the story and try to understand their meanings. Look at the choices that follow each word, and circle the one that reveals the correct meaning of the word as it is used in the story.

1 peak
   a the quietest time
   (b) the busiest time
   c the lowest point

2 stared
   a began
   b looked at for a long time
   c climbed

3 vineyard
   a house
   b garage
   c field of grape plants

4 drone
   a constant noise
   b unmanned plane
   c male bee

5 recover
  a feel better
  b hide
  c hurt

6 instinctively
  a quickly without thinking
  b slowly with thought
  c carefully

7 ached
  a a feeling of pain or loss
  b a feeling of relief
  c a feeling of relaxation

8 savoring
  a taking pleasure in
  b feeling sad about
  c putting aside

9 startled
  a sleepy
  b surprised
  c curious

10 nervous
  a relaxed
  b brave
  c uneasy

11 gladly
  a angrily
  b happily
  c sadly

12 shack
  a a small wooden building
  b a palace
  c a piece of land

Read the following lines from the story. What can you infer about character, setting, plot, or theme? Write your answer on the line below.

1 Ito, the strawberry share-cropper, did not smile. (lines 1–2)

He was sad that the season was ending, and he wouldn't have work.

2 As we drove away, I felt a lump in my throat. (line 59)

3 . . . Papà's face turn pale as he looked down the road. (lines 99–100)

4 I sat at the table across from Roberto. . . . I did not want to look up and face him. (line 127–128)

5 I sat in an empty seat in the back. (lines 138–139)

6 For the rest of the reading period I kept getting angrier and angrier with myself. (lines 162–163)

3 Analyzing the Story: Sense Impressions

All the descriptions below appear in the story. Find the descriptions in the story and match them with a sense by writing each description in the chart. There may be more than one answer.

> soaked in sweat
> chewing on a handkerchief
> the drone of insects
> The dirty water ran down my arms.
> I watched Papà's face turn pale.
>
> The sun kept beating down.
> the buzzing insect
> the hot, dry dust
> The mountains swallowed the sun.

Touch	Taste	Smell	Sight	Sound
				the drone of insects

Pair Discussion   With a partner, compare what you have written in your charts. Correct any mistakes you find. Then discuss how each description makes you feel.

4 Writing

Read the writing ideas that follow. Your instructor may make specific assignments or ask you to choose one of these:

1 Imagine you are picking strawberries in July. Describe the scene around you, your feelings, and what you can see, hear, taste, or smell.
2 Have you ever met an understanding teacher like Mr. Lema? Describe the teacher. How did he or she affect your life?
3 Imagine what it would be like to move around as much as the narrator and his family did. How would you adjust to new schools, teachers, and friends? Create ten questions to interview a migrant worker. Supply the answers yourself or have a classmate answer your questions.
4 Imagine you are Panchito. Write a letter to Mr. Lema ten years after the story ends. Describe what your life has been like.

TAKE A CLOSER LOOK

1 Analyzing and Comparing

In each of the following sections, you are asked to think about and compare two of the stories in Part One.

"A Day's Wait" and "Thank You, Ma'm"

- Compare Hemingway's Schatz to Hughes's Roger. In what ways are the two boys alike? How are they different?
- How do the adults in both stories treat the boys?
- What do the adults gain from their experiences with the boys?

"A Day's Wait" and "The Circuit"

- Describe the difference between the lifestyles of Hemingway's Schatz and Jimenez's Panchito.
- Describe the life lesson each boy learns. What did Schatz in "A Day's Wait" learn? What did Panchito in "The Circuit" learn?
- Compare Hemingway's Schatz and Jimenez's Panchito. How are they similar? How are they different? Could they become friends if they met someday? Give some reasons for your answer.

"Thank You, Ma'm" and "The Circuit"

- What advice would Panchito, the narrator in "The Circuit," give to Roger if he saw him steal the woman's purse?
- Compare the relationship each boy, Panchito and Roger, has with his father. What are the similarities? What are the differences?

2 Freewriting

Fear is a theme in each of the stories in Part One. For 15 minutes, write about fear as it occurs in the stories. What kinds of fears do the characters have? How do they deal with them? Which character do you understand best? Why?

When you have finished writing, exchange papers with a classmate and discuss your reactions.

B WORDS FREQUENTLY CONFUSED

Idioms and Expressions Review

Some people confuse English words that have similar pronunciations (homonyms) but different meanings, such as *too, to, two*; and *there, their, they're*. Other words are sometimes misused because they closely resemble one another in either spelling or meaning. For example,

thought (noun or verb)
though (conjunction)
Though he never called her, he often **thought** about her.

In Part One, there are many words that could be confused if not properly understood. Study the following list. Then choose ten pairs of words from the list and write sentences that clearly show the different meanings. You may use your dictionary.

From "A Day's Wait"

bear   noun: a large furry animal (such as a polar bear)

bare   adjective: unclothed, untrimmed (a bare arm or an empty refrigerator)

attach   verb: to connect to (Attach the document to the email)

detach   verb: to remove from (detach the plug from the wall socket)

die   verb: to expire (The butterfly may die.)

dead   adjective: no longer living (The butterfly is dead.)

read (pronounced *reed*)   verb: to look at and understand a book or paper (to read the novel)

read (pronounced *red*)   past tense of preceding verb (I read the novel yesterday.)

stare   verb: to look intently at someone or something (to stare at your friend)

stair   noun: a step (to sit on the stair)

heard   verb: past tense of *hear* (I heard the noise.)

herd   noun: a group of cattle (a herd of cows or sheep)

From "Thank You, Ma'm"

sat   verb: past tense of *sit* (sat on the steps)

set verb: to place or put (to set the table)

wait verb: to stay, pass time (They wait every morning for the bus.)

weigh verb: to determine the heaviness of an object (to weigh the meat on a scale)

weight noun: the measure (the weight of the meat)

woman singular noun: one female (a woman working)

women plural noun: two or more females (several women working)

teach verb: to instruct (to teach a class)

learn verb: to absorb instruction (The students learn.)

From "The Circuit"

peak noun: the top, the busiest time (The mountain peak was cloudy.) (It was the peak of rush hour traffic.)

peek verb: to take a quick look (I peek at the sleeping baby.)

break verb: destroy, damage (Don't break your leg!)

noun: to stop doing something for a short time (We took a coffee break.)

brake verb: stop quickly (You should brake for animals.)

noun: part of a vehicle that lets you stop (I stepped on the brake to stop the car.)

week noun: seven days (We were in Paris for a week.)

weak adjective: not strong (The patient was weak after the surgery.)

weight noun: how much something or someone weighs (She gained a lot of weight on vacation.)

bought verb: past tense of *buy* (They bought a lottery ticket and won!)

brought verb: past tense of *bring* (They brought their dogs to the party.)

tears noun: water in your eyes from crying (Her tears made me sad.)

tears verb: pulls off, pulls apart (He tears up the love letter and throws it away.)

loose adjective: not tight (She had lost so much weight that her pants were loose.)

lose verb: to not keep something in your possession (Be careful with your wallet or you will lose it!)

quit verb: to stop doing something (He quit his job.)

quite adverb: completely, entirely (The children are quite well-behaved.)

quiet adjective: to be silent, not noisy (I love to read in a quiet room.)

C SPELLING

Forming the Past Tense of Regular Verbs

In "Thank You, Ma'm" Roger tries to steal money from Mrs. Luella Bates Washington Jones. It never *occurred* to him to ask. Does it seem strange to you that we double the *r* in *occur* to form the past tense but not the *r* in *care*? The following are patterns that may help you remember the spelling of past tense regular verbs.

1 The verb *care* is a one-syllable word that ends in the vowel *e*. As in *hope* or *date*, the past tense is formed by adding the letter *d* to the root word: *cared, hoped, dated.*

2 *Occur* is a two-syllable word, and the accent (or stress) is on the second syllable. For all two-syllable words with second-syllable accents, we double the final consonant to form the past tense: *occur, occurred*; *prefer, preferred.*

3 If, however, the accent is on the first syllable, the past tense is formed by simply adding *-ed: listen, listened; offer, offered.*

4 For one-syllable words, we double the final letter to add *-ed* if the last letter is preceded by one vowel: *stop, stopped; top, topped.*

5 If a one-syllable word contains two vowels preceding the final letter, the past is formed just by adding *-ed: rain, rained; stain, stained.*

6 What about one-syllable words that end in two consonants, such as *walk* or *talk*? Just add *-ed.*

To see if you understand the patterns, practice by forming the past tense of the following:

WORDS THAT END IN *E*	
cope	
spare	
dine	

ONE-SYLLABLE WORDS WITH ONE VOWEL PRECEDING THE FINAL CONSONANT	
rob	
sob	
plan	

One-Syllable Words with Two Vowels Preceding the Final Consonant

stain	_____
fool	_____
wait	_____

Two-Syllable Words That Stress the First Syllable

offer	_____
happen	_____
open	_____

Two-Syllable Words That Stress the Second Syllable

control	_____
regret	_____
admit	_____

Words That End in Two Consonants

start	_____
fold	_____
warn	_____

D REVIEW TEST

Some of the following sentences are correct; in others, there are errors in the use of articles, prepositions, verb tense, adjectives, and adverbs. If you think the sentence is correct, write the letter *C* in the space below each sentence. If the sentence is incorrect, underline the error(s) and rewrite the sentence correctly. For example,

INCORRECT: She should have <u>saw</u> the car coming.

CORRECT: She should have **seen** the car coming.

1 The life isn't always easy, especially when we are studying a new language.

_____

2 We could have went to a better restaurant.

_____

3 Since I arrived to United States, I will enjoy many new experiences.

_____

4 Because we are learning English, we have read a number of short stories.

_____

5 It is necessary to drive careful, especially on highways.

_____

6 Katie had known rarely any rich people.

_____

7 I have seen seldom him in the supermarket.

_____

8 Everything at the wedding had went smooth.

_____

9 Schatz thought he would soon die in his bed.

_____

10 Mama went never anywhere without her cooking pot.

_____

11 My birthday is in June 25.

_____

12 I want to buy a pens.

_____

13 Roger was poor child in a story "Thank You, Ma'm."

_____

14 The flower smells sweet.

_____

15 You don't look good. Are you tired?

_____

16 She plays the piano well but she sings bad.

_____

17 Last summer we had swam almost every day.

_____

18 My father, who is a reporter, has known many famous people.

_____

19 Mrs. Jones asked Roger, "Aren't you ashamed with yourself?"

_____

20 She grabbed him on the neck and dragged him in the street.

21 We worked hard to the summer.

22 Students like to read stories about a adventurous heroes.

23 Anna well played the trumpet.

24 Panchito was impressed on what his teacher told him.

25 The story "The Circuit" is set at the United States.

WEBQUEST

Find more information about the topics in Part One by going on the Internet. Go to www.cambridge.org/discoveringfiction/wq and follow the instructions for doing a WebQuest. Have fun. Enjoy the quest!

PART TWO

The Unexpected Twist

LIFE IS full of surprises. How many times have you been amazed by the turn of events in your own life and the lives of your acquaintances? You were sure, for example, that your best friend would marry the girl next door, only to learn that he eloped with someone he just met. Or you're deep into that mystery novel; you think you can name the murderer. Then you get to the end of the story. You're astounded to find out that the least suspicious character is really the guilty one.

This literary device, used by most writers of suspense novels, is called the "unexpected twist" or the "surprise ending." O. Henry, the famous American author, never failed to shock his readers by his totally unpredictable endings, as you'll discover in "The Last Leaf." If you read the following stories carefully, you'll find some hints that the authors give to indicate that a surprise is coming. Look for these clues.

CHAPTER 4

The Last Leaf

O. Henry (William Sydney Porter)

A Preparing to Read

1 Think Before You Read

Answer the following questions before you read the story:

1 Greenwich Village is a section in the lower part of New York City where many aspiring artists have lived. What else do you know about "the Village"? What is it famous for now?

2 In your opinion, what constitutes a masterpiece?

3 Have you ever read a story in which a person made a great sacrifice either for a career or for another human being?

4 In the fourth paragraph of the story, the author describes pneumonia as though the disease were a person. This device is called personification. As you read, see if you can find other examples of personification.

5 You will also see references to items that are no longer used very often. People generally used a *chafing dish* to warm up food, whereas now we have the microwave. Do you know what *bishop's sleeves* are? Have you heard of *ragtime*?

2 Literary Term: Surprise Ending

The **surprise ending** is, as the term indicates, an ending that is totally unexpected. O. Henry is so famous for this type of ending that it is often called "the O. Henry ending." Other short-story writers have followed his example, especially American authors like Shirley Jackson and Edith Wharton.

Prepare yourself for a shock when you get to the conclusion of "The Last Leaf."

3 Idioms and Expressions

You will find these idioms and expressions in the story:

fair game something easy to conquer	**fibbertigibbet** flighty, frivolous person
dunderhead stupid person	**make up her mind** make a decision

B THE STORY

About the Author

William Sydney Porter (1862–1910) lived a tragic but adventurous life. He was born in Greensboro, North Carolina, where he worked as a pharmacist. Then he drifted off to Texas, where he met and eloped with his future wife. After their marriage, Porter worked as a bank teller but was accused of embezzling funds. Fearful of being convicted of a crime he said he did not commit, he fled to Central America. There he met other fugitives, worked on ranches as a cowboy, and gathered material that he later used in his short stories. Learning that his wife was seriously ill, Porter returned to the United States to stand trial. He was found guilty and sentenced to five years in prison. While in jail, Porter wrote and published 12 short stories under the pen name O. Henry. There are many versions of why he adopted that name. The most popular one is that he overheard the wife of the warden, whose first name was Henry, call out to her husband, "Oh, Henry."

While he was in prison, O. Henry's wife died. On his release, the bereaved husband decided to begin a new life in New York and settled in Greenwich Village. O. Henry enjoyed life in the city and became a famous writer. His short stories are noted for their surprise endings, as you will see when you read "The Last Leaf," which is part of a collection called *The Trimmed Lamp*, published in 1907.

The Last Leaf

In a little district west of Washington Square the streets have run crazy and broken themselves into small strips called "places." These "places" make strange angles and curves. One street crosses itself a time or two. An artist once discovered a valuable possibility in this street. Suppose
5 a collector with a bill for paints, paper and canvas should, in traversing this route, suddenly meet himself coming back, without a cent having been paid on account!

So, to quaint old Greenwich Village the art people soon came prowling, hunting for north windows and eighteenth-century gables and
10 Dutch attics and low rents. Then they imported some pewter mugs and a chafing dish or two from Sixth Avenue, and became a "colony."

At the top of a squatty, three-story brick Sue and Johnsy had their studio. "Johnsy" was familiar for Joanna. One was from Maine; the other from California. They had met at the table d'hôte of an Eighth
15 Street "Delmonico's," and found their tastes in art, chicory salad, and bishop sleeves so congenial that the joint studio resulted.

That was in May. In November a cold, unseen stranger, whom the doctors called Pneumonia, stalked about the colony, touching one here and there with his icy fingers. Over on the east side this ravager strode
20 boldly, smiting his victims by scores, but his feet trod slowly through the maze of the narrow and moss-grown "places."

Mr. Pneumonia was not what you would call a chivalric old gentleman. A mite of a little woman with blood thinned by California zephyrs was hardly fair game for the red-fisted, short-breathed old duffer. But Johnsy
25 he smote; and she lay, scarcely moving, on her painted iron bedstead, looking through the small Dutch windowpanes at the blank side of the next brick house.

One morning the busy doctor invited Sue into the hallway with a shaggy, gray eyebrow.
30 "She has one chance in – let us say, ten," he said, as he shook down

the mercury in his clinical thermometer. "And that chance is for her to want to live. This way people have of lining-up on the side of the undertaker makes the entire pharmacopoeia look silly. Your little lady has made up her mind that she's not going to get well. Has she anything on her mind?"

"She – she wanted to paint the Bay of Naples some day," said Sue.

"Paint? – bosh! Has she anything on her mind worth thinking about twice – a man, for instance?"

"A man?" said Sue. "Is a man worth – but, no, doctor; there is nothing of the kind."

"Well, it is the weakness, then," said the doctor. "I will do all that science, so far as it may filter through my efforts, can accomplish. But whenever my patient begins to count the carriages in her funeral procession I subtract 50 per cent from the curative power of medicines. If you will get her to ask one question about the new winter styles in cloak sleeves, I will promise you a one-in-five chance for her, instead of one in ten."

After the doctor had gone, Sue went into the workroom and cried a Japanese napkin to a pulp. Then she swaggered into Johnsy's room with her drawing board, whistling ragtime.

Johnsy lay, scarcely making a ripple under the bedclothes, with her face toward the window. Sue stopped whistling, thinking she was asleep.

She arranged her board and began a pen-and-ink drawing to illustrate a magazine story. Young artists must pave their way to Art by drawing pictures for magazine stories that young authors write to pave their way to Literature.

As Sue was sketching a pair of elegant horseshow riding trousers and a monocle on the figure of the hero, an Idaho cowboy, she heard a low sound, several times repeated. She went quickly to the bedside.

Johnsy's eyes were open wide. She was looking out the window and counting – counting backward.

"Twelve," she said, and a little later "eleven"; and then "ten," and "nine"; and then "eight" and "seven," almost together.

Sue looked solicitously out of the window. What was there to count? There was only a bare, dreary yard to be seen, and the blank side of the brick house twenty feet away. An old, old ivy vine, gnarled and decayed at the roots, climbed half way up the brick wall. The cold breath of autumn had stricken its leaves from the vine until its skeleton branches clung, almost bare, to the crumbling bricks.

"What is it, dear?" asked Sue.

"Six," said Johnsy, in almost a whisper. "They're falling faster now. Three days ago there were almost a hundred. It made my head ache to count them. But now it's easy. There goes another one. There are only five left now."

"Five what, dear? Tell your Sudie."

"Leaves. On the ivy vine. When the last one falls I must go, too. I've known that for three days. Didn't the doctor tell you?"

"Oh, I never heard of such nonsense," complained Sue, with magnificent scorn. "What have old ivy leaves to do with your getting well? And you used to love that vine so, you naughty girl. Don't be a goosey. Why, the doctor told me this morning that your chances for getting well real soon were – let's see exactly what he said – he said the chances were ten to one! Why, that's almost as good a chance as we have in New York when we ride on the street cars or walk past a new building. Try to take some broth now, and let Sudie go back to her drawing, so she can sell the editor man with it, and buy port wine for her sick child, and pork chops for her greedy self."

"You needn't get any more wine," said Johnsy, keeping her eyes fixed out the window. "There goes another. No, I don't want any broth. That leaves just four. I want to see the last one fall before it gets dark. Then I'll go, too."

"Johnsy, dear," said Sue, bending over her, "will you promise me to keep your eyes closed, and not look out the window until I am done working? I must hand those drawings in by tomorrow. I need the light, or I would draw the shade down."

"Couldn't you draw in the other room?" asked Johnsy, coldly.

"I'd rather be here by you," said Sue. "Besides, I don't want you to keep looking at those silly ivy leaves."

"Tell me as soon as you have finished," said Johnsy, closing her eyes, and lying white and still as a fallen statue, "because I want to see the last one fall. I'm tired of waiting. I'm tired of thinking. I want to turn loose my hold on everything, and go sailing down, down, just like one of those poor, tired leaves."

"Try to sleep," said Sue. "I must call Behrman up to be my model for the old hermit miner. I'll not be gone a minute. Don't try to move 'til I come back."

Old Behrman was a painter who lived on the ground floor beneath them. He was past sixty and had a Michael Angelo's Moses beard curling down from the head of a satyr along the body of an imp. Behrman was a failure in art. Forty years he had wielded the brush without getting near enough to touch the hem of his Mistress's robe. He had been always about to paint a masterpiece, but had never yet begun it. For several years he had painted nothing except now and then a daub in the line of commerce or advertising. He earned a little by serving as a model to those young artists in the colony who could not pay the price of a professional. He drank gin to excess, and still talked of his coming masterpiece. For the rest he was a fierce little old man, who scoffed terribly at softness in any one, and who regarded himself as especial

120 mastiff-in-waiting to protect the two young artists in the studio above.

Sue found Behrman smelling strongly of juniper berries in his dimly lighted den below. In one corner was a blank canvas on an easel that had been waiting there for twenty-five years to receive the first line of the masterpiece. She told him of Johnsy's fancy, and how she feared she
125 would, indeed, light and fragile as a leaf herself, float away, when her slight hold upon the world grew weaker.

Old Behrman, with his red eyes plainly streaming, shouted his contempt and derision for such idiotic imaginings.

"Vass!" he cried. "Is dere people in de world mit der foolishness
130 to die because leafs dey drop off from a confounded vine? I haf not heard of such a thing. No, I will not bose as a model for your fool hermitdunderhead. Vy do you allow dot silly pusiness to come in der brain of her? Ach, dot poor leetle Miss Yohnsy."

"She is very ill and weak," said Sue, "and the fever has left her mind
135 morbid and full of strange fancies. Very well, Mr. Behrman, if you do not care to pose for me, you needn't. But I think you are a horrid old – old flibbertigibbet."

"You are just like a woman!" yelled Behrman. "Who said I will not bose? Go on. I come mit you. For half an hour I haf peen trying to say
140 dot I am ready to bose. Gott! Dis is not any blace in which one so goot as Miss Yohnsy shall lie sick. Some day I vill baint a masterpiece, and ve shall all go away. Gott! Yes."

Johnsy was sleeping when they went upstairs. Sue pulled the shade down to the window-sill, and motioned Behrman into the other room.
145 In there they peered out the window fearfully at the ivy vine. Then they looked at each other for a moment without speaking. A persistent, cold rain was falling, mingled with snow. Behrman, in his old blue shirt, took his seat as the hermit miner on an upturned kettle for a rock.

When Sue awoke from an hour's sleep the next morning she found
150 Johnsy with dull, wide-open eyes staring at the drawn green shade.

"Pull it up; I want to see," she ordered, in a whisper.

Wearily Sue obeyed.

But, lo! after the beating rain and fierce gusts of wind that had endured through the livelong night, there yet stood out against the brick
155 wall one ivy leaf. It was the last on the vine. Still dark green near its stem, but with its serrated edges tinted with the yellow of dissolution and decay, it hung bravely from a branch some twenty feet above the ground.

"It is the last one," said Johnsy. "I thought it would surely fall during
160 the night. I heard the wind. It will fall today, and I shall die at the same time."

"Dear, dear!" said Sue, leaning her worn face down to the pillow, "think of me, if you won't think of yourself. What would I do?"

But Johnsy did not answer. The lonesomest thing in all the world is a soul when it is making ready to go on its mysterious, far journey. The fancy seemed to possess her more strongly as one by one the ties that bound her to friendship and to earth were loosed.

The day wore away, and even through the twilight they could see the lone ivy leaf clinging to its stem against the wall. And then, with the coming of the night the north wind was again loosed, while the rain still beat against the windows and pattered down from the low Dutch eaves.

When it was light enough Johnsy, the merciless, commanded that the shade be raised.

The ivy leaf was still there.

Johnsy lay for a long time looking at it. And then she called to Sue, who was stirring her chicken broth over the gas stove.

"I've been a bad girl, Sudie," said Johnsy. "Something has made that last leaf stay there to show me how wicked I was. It is a sin to want to die. You may bring me a little broth now, and some milk with a little port in it, and – no; bring me a hand-mirror first, and then pack some pillows about me, and I will sit up and watch you cook."

An hour later she said:

"Sudie, some day I hope to paint the Bay of Naples."

The doctor came in the afternoon, and Sue had an excuse to go into the hallway as he left.

"Even chances," said the doctor, taking Sue's thin, shaking hand in his. "With good nursing you'll win. And now I must see another case I have downstairs. Behrman, his name is – some kind of an artist, I believe. Pneumonia, too. He is an old, weak man, and the attack is acute. There is no hope for him; but he goes to the hospital today to be made more comfortable."

The next day the doctor said to Sue: "She's out of danger. You've won. Nutrition and care now – that's all."

And that afternoon Sue came to the bed where Johnsy lay, contentedly knitting a very blue and very useless woollen shoulder scarf, and put one arm around her, pillows and all.

"I have something to tell you, white mouse," she said. "Mr. Behrman died of pneumonia today in the hospital. He was ill only two days. The janitor found him on the morning of the first day in his room downstairs helpless with pain. His shoes and clothing were wet through and icy cold. They couldn't imagine where he had been on such a dreadful night. And then they found a lantern, still lighted, and a ladder that had been dragged from its place, and some scattered brushes, and a palette with green and yellow colors mixed on it, and – look out the window, dear, at the last ivy leaf on the wall. Didn't you wonder why it never fluttered or moved when the wind blew? Ah, darling, it's Behrman's masterpiece – he painted it there the night that the last leaf fell."

C UNDERSTANDING THE STORY

1 Reading Comprehension

Answer these questions to determine how well you understood the story:

1 The story is set in New York's Greenwich Village, at one time famous for its art colony. How do we know that the author is familiar with his setting?
2 Why does Johnsy feel she is fated to die?
3 Describe Mr. Behrman.
4 What was Mr. Behrman's masterpiece?
5 At what point in the story do you begin to think that Mr. Behrman will help Johnsy?
6 What was the ending of "The Last Leaf"? How did you feel when you reached the end of the story?

2 Guessing Meaning from Context

Read each of the following sentences. The words in **bold** are in the story. Find the words in the story and try to understand their meanings. Write a synonym for each word in the space provided at the end of the sentence.

1 The hiker had to **traverse** many paths before he found a stream to wash his face and hands. ___*walk across*___

2 That **quaint** little house is a contrast to all the modern buildings surrounding it. _____

3 Cats often **prowl** all night, looking for food. _____

4 When we go to a party, we expect to meet **congenial** people.

_____

5 Frankenstein's monster was a **ravager** who roamed the countryside, causing widespread damage. _____

6 An epidemic often **smites** children and old people. _____

7 In medieval times, knights were expected to be **chivalric**.

_____

8 The conceited football player **swaggered** off the field after having made the winning touchdown. _____

9 Sue's care of Johnsy showed how **solicitous** she was for her friend's welfare. _____

10 People who are afraid of being robbed sometimes have a **mastiff** to protect them. _____

11 Johnsy had a **morbid** conviction that she would die when the last leaf fell from the vine. _____

12 Years ago, many immigrants came to America thinking that the streets were **paved** with gold. _____

13 A saw, like a leaf, has edges that are **serrated**. _____

14 Parents should never **scoff at** their children's ambitions even if they seem ridiculous. _____

15 Most women like to look **elegant** when attending a dinner party.

_____

3 Grammar: Infinitives and Gerunds

In "The Last Leaf," O. Henry uses many infinitives and gerunds. Here are some examples from the story:

INFINITIVES	GERUNDS
want **to see**	tired **of waiting**
try **to sleep**	go **sailing**
hope **to plant**	without **speaking**

Infinitives are formed by using *to* + the present tense of a verb, for example, *to run*. Never form an infinitive by adding *to* to the past tense.

INCORRECT: to walked
CORRECT: **to walk**

Gerunds are formed by placing *-ing* at the end of a verb, for example, *running*.

Infinitives and gerunds are called verbals because they look like verbs but function as other parts of speech. Infinitives function as nouns, adjectives, or adverbs. Gerunds function as nouns. Certain verbs must be followed by infinitives – not gerunds. You cannot say, for example: I want *seeing* that film. You must say: I want **to see** that film.

Here are some other verbs that require infinitives:

hope	pretend	need	seem
decide	refuse	offer	
agree	expect	promise	

Other verbs are always followed by gerunds, such as *go* (go swimming) and the verbs listed here:

avoid	delay	consider	discuss
mind	quit	dislike	
finish	enjoy	keep	

Do not say, for example: I enjoy *to dance*. Use the gerund: I enjoy **dancing**.

Note: Although you must use a gerund with *dislike*, you may use either a gerund or an infinitive with *like*. You may say: I like **to dance** or I like **dancing**.

Application   Now complete this exercise by using the correct form of the verbal (infinitive or gerund).

1 I lost my bracelet. Will you keep _____*looking*_____ (look) for it?

2 Johnsy wanted _____ (paint) the Bay of Naples.

3 Do you mind _____ (turn) off the TV?

4 Both Sue and Johnsy enjoyed _____ (live) in Greenwich Village.

5 Mr. Behrman offered _____ (help) the sick Johnsy.

6 I dislike _____ (stay) out late on weeknights.

7 Many restaurants won't allow customers _____ (smoke).

8 I need _____ (buy) a new chair for my living room.

9 Mr. Behrman hoped some day _____ (produce) a masterpiece.

10 In fact, he expected _____ (do) it very soon.

11 It seems _____ (be) cloudy every day.

12 When you finish _____ (work), let's go out to the movies.

13 We decided _____ (stay) home for the Thanksgiving holidays.

14 That way we can avoid _____ (travel) in the heavy traffic.

15 I promise _____ (go) on a diet soon.

16 Sue refused _____ (believe) that Johnsy would die.

17 Shall we consider _____ (hire) an artist to illustrate our book?

18 Why do you delay _____ (make) a decision?

19 Let's agree _____ (wait) until tomorrow before telling her the bad news.

20 Mr. Behrman promised _____ (pose) for Sue's picture.

4 Editing

Correct the misuse of infinitives and gerunds in the following paragraph.

I have always enjoyed to read stories with a surprise ending. I dislike to know what will happen before I finish to read the ending. I need having an unexpected twist, and I refuse selecting any more stories by authors who decide giving the reader too many hints. O. Henry was a master who delayed to tell the outcome of the plot until the very last sentence. I hope finding other authors like O. Henry.

D THINKING CRITICALLY

1 Discussing the Story

Discuss the following questions with a partner, in a small group, or with the whole class:

1 Do you know of any cases in life or in literature in which a person lost the will to live? Do you think a desire to survive can overcome even a fatal illness?
2 Discuss the friendship between Sue and Johnsy. Give examples that prove Sue's loyalty.
3 In what way is the setting important to the story? Suppose Johnsy had become ill in the spring or the summer?
4 How does the ending prove that Mr. Behrman was a great artist?
5 What other examples in the story indicate Mr. Behrman's deep feeling for Sue and Johnsy?

2 Making Inferences

> Authors often write something that is intended to have more than one meaning. While you read, look for meanings that are not explicitly stated – these are inferences. Making inferences will help you enjoy the reading on a different level. The story now has deeper significance, and you will have a better understanding of it.

Read the following lines from the story. What can you infer about character, setting, plot, or theme? Write your answer on the line below.

1 "She has one chance in . . . ten." (line 30)

She is likely to die.

2 Then she swaggered into Johnsy's room with her drawing board, whistling ragtime. (lines 49–50)

3 "When the last one falls, I must go, too." (line 77)

4 He had been always about to paint a masterpiece, but had never yet begun it. (line 112–113)

5 "Sudie, someday I hope to paint the Bay of Naples." (line 183)

3 Analyzing the Story: Surprise Ending

Look back at the Literary Term on page 57. O. Henry's short stories usually have surprise endings. Think about how the reader expects the story to end. How is the actual ending different? On the lines below, write the words and phrases from the story that make you think Johnsy is going to die. Then at the bottom, write the surprise ending.

A mite of a little woman . . . hardly fair game . . . (lines 23–24)

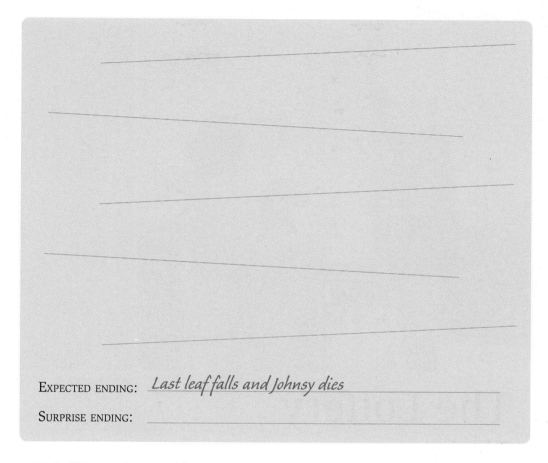

EXPECTED ENDING: *Last leaf falls and Johnsy dies*

SURPRISE ENDING:

Pair Discussion   With a partner, compare what you have written in your charts. Correct any mistakes you find. Discuss any differences you find. Were you surprised by the ending? Did anything in the story help you guess it?

4 Writing

Read the writing ideas that follow. Your instructor may make specific assignments or ask you to choose one of these:

1 In the fourth paragraph of the story, O. Henry describes pneumonia as though the disease were a person. Write a paragraph in which you also use personification. You might wish to describe a season, an old house, flowers, falling leaves, or something else.
2 Write a dialogue between Johnsy and Sue a year later, on the anniversary of Mr. Behrman's death.
3 Write an original story with a surprise ending.
4 Retell a story from your native country that contains the theme of someone making a sacrifice for another.
5 Compare Johnsy's attitude toward her chances for survival with Schatz's in "A Day's Wait." Cite specific examples from each story.

CHAPTER 5

The Lottery

Shirley Jackson

A PREPARING TO READ

1 Think Before You Read

Answer the following questions:

1 What is a lottery?
2 Have you ever bought a lottery ticket? Why did you buy it?
3 Look at the story "The Circuit" and think about the discussion of sense impressions as you read this story.
4 Many writers use surprise endings in their stories. Why is such an ending effective?

2 Literary Term: Irony

Irony results from a difference between reality and appearance. We say there is irony in a situation when something that happens is the opposite of what we expect. For example, pretend you are in a gambling casino and have only one dollar left. You give your last dollar to a waiter as a tip. He puts it in a slot machine and wins the jackpot. It is ironic that you gave away your last dollar, which was a winner. Irony makes us aware of how unpredictable life can be.

3 Idioms and Expressions

You will find these idioms and expressions in the story:

sat uneasily was a new experience, didn't feel right	**a good sport** someone who reacts well to a situation
give me a hand help me	**clean forgot** completely forgot something
get this over with finish doing something unpleasant	
A sudden hush fell on the crowd. It became quiet. People stopped talking.	

B THE STORY

About the Author

Shirley Jackson (1919–1965) was born in San Francisco, California, but spent her college years in the Northeast. After her marriage, she moved to Vermont and raised four children.

Jackson's writing ranges from humorous stories and novels, including a memoir of her life with her children called *Life among the Savages*, to psychological and horror stories such as "The Lottery." Some of her stories have been adapted into movies.

An important element in Jackson's style is her ability to use minor details and casual conversation to convey powerful images. Her language is carefully chosen to heighten the impact of the horror. What may appear ordinary and commonplace on the surface is intended to produce a memorable effect.

"The Lottery" was published in 1948 in *The New Yorker* magazine, and it created a great deal of attention. Many readers and literary critics consider the story symbolic of World War II.

The Lottery

The morning of June 27th was clear and sunny, with the fresh warmth of a full-summer day; the flowers were blossoming profusely and the grass was richly green. The people of the village began to gather in the square, between the post office and the bank, around ten o'clock; in
5 some towns there were so many people that the lottery took two days and had to be started on June 26th, but in this village, where there were only about three hundred people, the whole lottery took less than two hours, so it could begin at ten o'clock in the morning and still be through in time to allow the villagers to get home for noon dinner.
10 The children assembled first, of course. School was recently over for the summer, and the feeling of liberty sat uneasily on most of them; they tended to gather together quietly for a while before they broke into boisterous play, and their talk was still of the classroom and the teacher, of books and reprimands. Bobby Martin had already stuffed his pockets
15 full of stones, and the other boys soon followed his example, selecting the smoothest and roundest stones; Bobby and Harry Jones and Dickie Delacroix – the villagers pronounced this name "Dellacroy" – eventually made a great pile of stones in one corner of the square and guarded it against the raids of the other boys. The girls stood aside, talking among
20 themselves, looking over their shoulders at the boys, and the very small children rolled in the dust or clung to the hands of their older brothers or sisters.

Soon the men began to gather, surveying their own children, speaking of planting and rain, tractors and taxes. They stood together, away from
25 the pile of stones in the corner, and their jokes were quiet and they smiled rather than laughed. The women, wearing faded house dresses and sweaters, came shortly after their menfolk. They greeted one another and exchanged bits of gossip as they went to join their husbands. Soon the women, standing by their husbands, began to call to their children,
30 and the children came reluctantly, having to be called four or five times. Bobby Martin ducked under his mother's grasping hand and ran,

laughing, back to the pile of stones. His father spoke up sharply, and Bobby came quickly and took his place between his father and his oldest brother.

35   The lottery was conducted – as were the square dances, the teenage club, the Halloween program – by Mr. Summers, who had time and energy to devote to civic activities. He was a round-faced, jovial man and he ran the coal business, and people were sorry for him, because he had no children and his wife was a scold. When he arrived in the square,
40 carrying the black wooden box, there was a murmur of conversation among the villagers and he waved and called, "Little late today, folks." The postmaster, Mr. Graves, followed him, carrying a three-legged stool, and the stool was put in the center of the square and Mr. Summers set the black box down on it. The villagers kept their distance, leaving a
45 space between themselves and the stool, and when Mr. Summers said, "Some of you fellows want to give me a hand?" there was a hesitation before two men, Mr. Martin and his oldest son, Baxter, came forward to hold the box steady on the stool while Mr. Summers stirred up the papers inside it.

50   The original paraphernalia for the lottery had been lost long ago, and the black box now resting on the stool had been put into use even before Old Man Warner, the oldest man in town, was born. Mr. Summers spoke frequently to the villagers about making a new box, but no one liked to upset even as much tradition as was represented by the black box.
55 There was a story that the present box had been made with some pieces of the box that had preceded it, the one that had been constructed when the first people settled down to make a village here. Every year, after the lottery, Mr. Summers began talking again about a new box, but every year the subject was allowed to fade off without anything's
60 being done. The black box grew shabbier each year; by now it was no longer completely black but splintered badly along one side to show the original wood color, and in some places faded or stained.

    Mr. Martin and his oldest son, Baxter, held the black box securely on the stool until Mr. Summers had stirred the papers thoroughly with his
65 hand. Because so much of the ritual had been forgotten or discarded, Mr. Summers had been successful in having slips of paper substituted for the chips of wood that had been used for generations. Chips of wood, Mr. Summers had argued, had been all very well when the village was tiny, but now that the population was more than three hundred and
70 likely to keep on growing, it was necessary to use something that would fit more easily into the black box. The night before the lottery, Mr. Summers and Mr. Graves made up the slips of paper and put them in the box, and it was then taken to the safe of Mr. Summers's coal company and locked up until Mr. Summers was ready to take it to the square next
75 morning. The rest of the year, the box was put away, sometimes one

place, sometimes another; it had spent one year in Mr. Graves's barn and another year underfoot in the post office, and sometimes it was set on a shelf in the Martin grocery and left there.

There was a great deal of fussing to be done before Mr. Summers declared the lottery open. There were lists to make up – heads of families, heads of households in each family, members of each household in each family. There was the proper swearing-in of Mr. Summers by the postmaster, as the official of the lottery; at one time, some people remembered, there had been a recital of some sort, performed by the official of the lottery, a perfunctory, tuneless chant that had been rattled off duly each year; some people believed that the official of the lottery used to stand just so when he said or sang it, others believed that he was supposed to walk among the people, but years and years ago this part of the ritual had been allowed to lapse. There had been, also, a ritual salute, which the official of the lottery had had to use in addressing each person who came up to draw from the box, but this also had changed with time, until now it was felt necessary only for the official to speak to each person approaching. Mr. Summers was very good at all this; in his clean white shirt and blue jeans, with one hand resting carelessly on the black box, he seemed very proper and important as he talked interminably to Mr. Graves and the Martins.

Just as Mr. Summers finally left off talking and turned to the assembled villagers, Mrs. Hutchinson came hurriedly along the path to the square, her sweater thrown over her shoulders, and slid into place in the back of the crowd. "Clean forgot what day it was," she said to Mrs. Delacroix, who stood next to her, and they both laughed softly. "Thought my old man was out back stacking wood," Mrs. Hutchinson went on, "and then I looked out the window and the kids were gone, and then I remembered it was the twenty-seventh and came arunning." She dried her hands on her apron, and Mrs. Delacroix said, "You're in time, though. They're still talking away up there."

Mrs. Hutchinson craned her neck to see through the crowd and found her husband and children standing near the front. She tapped Mrs. Delacroix on the arm as a farewell and began to make her way through the crowd. The people separated good-humoredly to let her through; two or three people said, in voices just loud enough to be heard across the crowd, "Here comes your Missus, Hutchinson," and "Bill, she made it after all." Mrs. Hutchinson reached her husband, and Mr. Summers, who had been waiting, said cheerfully, "Thought we were going to have to get on without you, Tessie." Mrs. Hutchinson said, grinning, "Wouldn't have me leave m'dishes in the sink, now would you, Joe?" and soft laughter ran through the crowd as the people stirred back into position after Mrs. Hutchinson's arrival.

"Well, now," Mr. Summers said soberly, "guess we better get started, get this over with, so's we can go back to work. Anybody ain't here?"

"Dunbar," several people said. "Dunbar, Dunbar."

Mr. Summers consulted his list. "Clyde Dunbar," he said. "That's right. He's broke his leg, hasn't he? Who's drawing for him?"

"Me, I guess," a woman said, and Mr. Summers turned to look at her.
125 "Wife draws for her husband," Mr. Summers said. "Don't you have a grown boy to do it for you, Janey?" Although Mr. Summers and everyone else in the village knew the answer perfectly well, it was the business of the official of the lottery to ask such questions formally. Mr. Summers waited with an expression of polite interest while Mrs. Dunbar answered.

130 "Horace's not but sixteen yet," Mrs. Dunbar said regretfully. "Guess I gotta fill in for the old man this year."

"Right," Mr. Summers said. He made a note on the list he was holding. Then he asked, "Watson boy drawing this year?"

135 A tall boy in the crowd raised his hand. "Here," he said. "I'm drawing for m'mother and me." He blinked his eyes nervously and ducked his head as several voices in the crowd said things like "Good fellow,
140 Jack," and "Glad to see your mother's got a man to do it."

"Well," Mr. Summers said, "guess that's everyone. Old Man Warner make it?"

"Here," a voice said and Mr. Summers
145 nodded.

> A sudden hush fell on the crowd as Mr. Summers cleared his throat and looked at the list. "All ready?" he called.

A sudden hush fell on the crowd as Mr. Summers cleared his throat and looked at the list. "All ready?" he called. "Now, I'll read the names – heads of families first – and the men come up and take a paper out of the box. Keep the paper folded in your hand without looking at it until
150 everyone has had a turn. Everything clear?"

The people had done it so many times that they only half listened to the directions; most of them were quiet, wetting their lips, not looking around. Then Mr. Summers raised one hand high and said, "Adams." A man disengaged himself from the crowd and came forward. "Hi, Steve,"
155 Mr. Summers said, and Mr. Adams said, "Hi, Joe." They grinned at one another humorlessly and nervously. Then Mr. Adams reached into the black box and took out a folded paper. He held it firmly by one corner as he turned and went hastily back to his place in the crowd, where he stood a little apart from his family, not looking down at his hand.

160 "Allen," Mr. Summers said. "Anderson . . . Bentham."

"Seems like there's no time at all between lotteries any more," Mrs. Delacroix said to Mrs. Graves in the back row. "Seems like we got through with the last one only last week."

"Time sure goes fast," Mrs. Graves said.
165 "Clark . . . Delacroix."

"There goes my old man," Mrs. Delacroix said. She held her breath while her husband went forward.

"Dunbar," Mr. Summers said, and Mrs. Dunbar went steadily to the box while one of the women said, "Go on, Janey," and another said, "There she goes."

"We're next," Mrs. Graves said. She watched while Mr. Graves came around from the side of the box, greeted Mr. Summers gravely, and selected a slip of paper from the box. By now, all through the crowd there were men holding the small folded papers in their large hands, turning them over and over nervously. Mrs. Dunbar and her two sons stood together, Mrs. Dunbar holding the slip of paper.

"Harburt . . . Hutchinson."

"Get up there, Bill," Mrs. Hutchinson said, and the people near her laughed.

"Jones."

"They do say," Mr. Adams said to Old Man Warner, who stood next to him, "that over in the north village they're talking of giving up the lottery."

Old Man Warner snorted. "Pack of crazy fools," he said. "Listening to the young folks, nothing's good enough for *them*. Next thing you know, they'll be wanting to go back to living in caves, nobody work any more, live *that* way for a while. Used to be a saying about 'Lottery in June, corn be heavy soon.' First thing you know, we'd all be eating stewed chickweed and acorns. There's *always* been a lottery," he added petulantly. "Bad enough to see young Joe Summers up there joking with everybody."

"Some places have already quit lotteries," Mrs. Adams said.

"Nothing but trouble in *that*," Old Man Warner said stoutly. "Pack of young fools."

"Martin." And Bobby Martin watched his father go forward. "Overdyke . . . Percy."

"I wish they'd hurry," Mrs. Dunbar said to her older son. "I wish they'd hurry."

"They're almost through," her son said.

"You get ready to run tell Dad," Mrs. Dunbar said.

Mr. Summers called his own name and then stepped forward precisely and selected a slip from the box. Then he called, "Warner."

"Seventy-seventh year I been in the lottery," Old Man Warner said as he went through the crowd. "Seventy-seventh time."

"Watson." The tall boy came awkwardly through the crowd. Someone said, "Don't be nervous, Jack," and Mr. Summers said, "Take your time, son."

"Zanini."

After that, there was a long pause, a breathless pause, until Mr. Summers, holding his slip of paper in the air, said, "All right, fellows." For a minute, no one moved, and then all the slips of paper were opened.

210 Suddenly, all women began to speak at once, saying, "Who is it?" "Who's got it?" "Is it the Dunbars?" "Is it the Watsons?" Then the voices began to say, "It's Hutchinson. It's Bill." "Bill Hutchinson's got it."

"Go tell your father," Mrs. Dunbar said to her older son.

People began to look around to see the Hutchinsons. Bill Hutchinson
215 was standing quiet, staring down at the paper in his hand. Suddenly, Tessie Hutchinson shouted to Mr. Summers, "You didn't give him time enough to take any paper he wanted. I saw you. It wasn't fair!"

"Be a good sport, Tessie," Mrs. Delacroix called, and Mrs. Graves said, "All of us took the same chance."

220 "Shut up, Tessie," Bill Hutchinson said.

"Well, everyone," Mr. Summers said, "that was done pretty fast, and now we've got to be hurrying a little more to get done in time." He consulted his next list. "Bill," he said, "you draw for the Hutchinson family. You got any other households in the Hutchinsons?"

225 "There's Don and Eva," Mrs. Hutchinson yelled. "Make *them* take their chance!"

"Daughters draw with their husbands' families, Tessie," Mr. Summers said gently. "You know that as well as anyone else."

"It wasn't fair," Tessie said.

230 "I guess not, Joe," Bill Hutchinson said regretfully. "My daughter draws with her husband's family, that's only fair. And I've got no other family except the kids."

"Then, as far as drawing for families is concerned, it's you," Mr. Summers said in explanation, "and as far as drawing for households is
235 concerned, that's you, too. Right?"

"Right," Bill Hutchinson said.

"How many kids, Bill?" Mr. Summers asked formally.

"Three," Bill Hutchinson said. "There's Bill, Jr., and Nancy, and little Dave. And Tessie and me."

240 "All right, then," Mr. Summers said. "Harry, you got their tickets back?"

Mr. Graves nodded and held up the slips of paper. "Put them in the box, then," Mr. Summers directed. "Take Bill's and put it in."

"I think we ought to start over," Mrs. Hutchinson said, as quietly as she could. "I tell you it wasn't *fair*. You didn't give him time enough to
245 choose. *Everybody* saw that."

Mr. Graves had selected the five slips and put them in the box, and he dropped all the papers but those onto the ground, where the breeze caught them and lifted them off.

"Listen, everybody," Mrs. Hutchinson was saying to the people
250 around her.

"Ready, Bill?" Mr. Summers said, "take the slips and keep them folded until each person has taken one. Harry, you help little Dave."

Mr. Graves took the hand of the little boy, who came willingly with him up to the box. "Take a paper out of the box, Davy," Mr. Summers said. Davy put his hand into the box and laughed. "Take just *one* paper," Mr. Summers said. "Harry, you hold it for him." Mr. Graves took the child's hand and removed the folded paper from the tight fist and held it while Dave stood next to him and looked up at him wonderingly.

"Nancy next," Mr. Summers said. Nancy was twelve, and her school friends breathed heavily as she went forward, switching her skirt, and took a slip daintily from the box. "Bill, Jr.," Mr. Summers said, and Billy, his face red and his feet overlarge, nearly knocked the box over as he got a paper out. "Tessie," Mr. Summers said. She hesitated for a minute, looking around defiantly, and then set her lips and went up to the box. She snatched a paper out and held it behind her.

"Bill," Mr. Summers said, and Bill Hutchinson reached into the box and felt around, bringing his hand out at last with the slip of paper in it.

The crowd was quiet. A girl whispered, "I hope it's not Nancy," and the sound of the whisper reached the edges of the crowd.

"It's not the way it used to be," Old Man Warner said clearly. "People ain't the way they used to be."

"All right," Mr. Summers said. "Open the papers. Harry, you open little Dave's."

Mr. Graves opened the slip of paper and there was a general sigh through the crowd as he held it up and everyone could see that it was blank. Nancy and Bill, Jr., opened theirs at the same time, and both beamed and laughed, turning around to the crowd and holding their slips of paper above their heads.

"Tessie," Mr. Summers said. There was a pause, and then Mr. Summers looked at Bill Hutchinson, and Bill unfolded his paper and showed it. It was blank.

"It's Tessie," Mr. Summers said, and his voice was hushed. "Show us her paper, Bill."

Bill Hutchinson went over to his wife and forced the slip of paper out of her hand. It had a black spot on it, the black spot Mr. Summers had made the night before with the heavy pencil in the coal-company office. Bill Hutchinson held it up, and there was a stir in the crowd.

"All right, folks," Mr. Summers said, "let's finish quickly."

Although the villagers had forgotten the ritual and lost the original black box, they still remembered to use stones. The pile of stones the boys had made earlier was ready; there were stones on the ground with the blowing scraps of paper that had come out of the box. Mrs. Delacroix selected a stone so large she had to pick it up with both hands and turned to Mrs. Dunbar. "Come on," she said. "Hurry up."

Mrs. Dunbar had small stones in both hands, and she said, gasping for breath, "I can't run at all. You'll have to go ahead and I'll catch up with you."

The children had stones already, and someone gave little Davy Hutchinson a few pebbles.

300   Tessie Hutchinson was in the center of a cleared space by now, and she held her hands out desperately as the villagers moved in on her. "It isn't fair," she said. A stone hit her on the side of the head.

     Old Man Warner was saying, "Come on, come on, everyone." Steve Adams was in the front of the crowd of villagers, with Mrs. Graves
305 beside him.

     "It isn't fair, it isn't right," Mrs. Hutchinson screamed, and then they were upon her.

C   UNDERSTANDING THE STORY

1 Reading Comprehension

Answer these questions to determine how well you understood the story:

1 At what time of year is the lottery held? What month?
2 Who is in charge of the lottery? Is anyone exempt from it?
3 Why isn't Mr. Dunbar present at the lottery drawing?
4 Why have some villages stopped having lotteries?
5 How does Old Man Warner feel about the lottery?
6 Who picks the paper with the black dot?
7 What is the lottery winner's prize?
8 Why does Mrs. Delacroix pick up a large stone?

2 Guessing Meaning from Context

The words in the list are in the story. Find the words in the story and try to understand their meanings. Write the appropriate word(s) in each sentence. Use each word only once.

profusely	petulantly	interminably	soberly
murmur	reprimand	hastily	craned
paraphernalia	scold	boisterous	snorted
perfunctory	splintered	jovial	

1 They _____*craned*_____ their necks to see the president in the motorcade.

2 The hikers carried all their _____ for the trip in their backpacks.

3 The lecture seemed _____ long, and many people dozed off.

4 You could hear the low _____ among the waiting crowd.

5 We were embarrassed to see the teacher _____ him in front of the whole class. Teachers shouldn't _____ students in public.

6 The wooden table was old and _____ from constant use.

7 The children were _____ as they ran out to play.

8 Don't be so unfriendly; try to be more _____.

9 The runners perspired _____ after they finished the marathon.

10 Our professor's _____ remarks before the exam made us more nervous.

11 The stubborn little girl looked at her father _____.

12 The pigs _____ as they followed the farmer around their sty.

13 The lawyer was very serious as she _____ questioned the potential jurors.

14 Because he was late, he _____ packed his clothes and creased everything.

3 Grammar: Roots, Prefixes, and Suffixes

Expanding your vocabulary is an important part of becoming fluent in a language. It is helpful to know the meanings of roots, prefixes, and suffixes in order to "attack" new vocabulary.

● Roots English is based on Latin, but many English words have been borrowed from the Greek, French, German, Italian, and Spanish languages.

● **Prefixes** Often, the definition of a word can be determined by knowing the meaning of a prefix. Prefixes are common in English; the following prefixes are frequently used to change the meanings of words:

ambi both	**mal, mis** badly
dis not, apart from	**pre** before
im, ir, il, in not	**re** again
inter between	**multi** *many*

Here is a list of additional prefixes:

ante before	**de** away
anti against	**intro, intra** inside
bene well	**sub** under
bi two	**syn, sym** same
circum around	**trans** across
co, com, col together, with	**un** not

● **Suffixes** Suffixes are added to the end of a root and, like prefixes, they change the meanings of words. For instance, the word *national* is made by adding -*al* to the root *nation*.

Application 1 The following roots will help you define new words. In addition to the sample words given, think of other words and write them on the lines.

auto	self	automobile, autocrat	*automatic*
bio	life	biology	
capit	head	capital	
ced	move	recede	
chron	time	chronicle	
corp	body	corporate	
cycle	circle	recycle	
derm	skin	epidermis	
dic, dict	say, word	predict, dictionary	
duc, duct	lead	conduct	

fac, fact make, do	facsimile _____
flect bend	reflect _____
geo earth	geography _____
graph write, record	autograph _____
homo same	homonym _____
log, logy study	biology _____
manu hand	manual _____
micro small	microcosm _____
mort death	mortal _____
peri around	periscope _____
phil love	Francophile _____
phon sound	phonograph _____
photo light	photograph _____
port carry	portable _____
psych mind	psychology _____
scop see	telescope _____
scrib, script write	prescription _____
soph wise	philosopher _____
spir breath	inspiration _____
tele far	telephone _____
terra earth	territory _____
therm heat	thermal _____
vene, vent come	convention _____

Application 2   For the following exercise, first enter the meaning of each word in the column on the left. Then use the prefixes listed in Application 1 to change the words. Enter the new words and their meanings in the column on the right.

	MEANING OF THE WORD	WORD WITH A PREFIX ADDED AND ITS MEANING
1. regular	*normal*	*irregular = not normal*
2. national		
3. action		
4. material		
5. respect		
6. existing		
7. conception		
8. legal		
9. complete		
10. adjust		
11. establish		
12. dexterous		
13. literate		

Application 3   For the exercise that follows, use the list of prefixes on page 81, but complete each entry as you did in Application 2.

	MEANING OF THE WORD	WORD WITH A PREFIX ADDED AND ITS MEANING
1. cycle	*wheeled vehicle*	*bicycle: two-wheeled vehicle*
2. compose		
3. marine		
4. operate		

5. continental _____ _____

6. diction _____ _____

7. appreciative _____ _____

8. navigate _____ _____

9. room _____ _____

10. virus _____ _____

11. passionate _____ _____

12. phonic _____ _____

13. social _____ _____

14. thesis _____ _____

Application 4 The suffixes in the following exercise will help you define new words. In addition to the sample words given, think of other words and write them on the lines.

al pertaining to, of, belonging to national, natural _____

ary pertaining to elementary _____

er, or one who, that which actor, winner _____

ful full of careful _____

ible, able able to reliable _____

ion, tion state of, result of creation _____

ious, tious state of anxious _____

ist one who does artist _____

less without, not having hopeless _____

Application 5 By looking carefully at the following words, you should be able to discover their meanings. Pay attention to the roots, prefixes, and suffixes, and write a definition for each word.

autobiography _____

circumnavigation _____

synonymous _____

unicycle _____

perspiration _____

geology _____

manufacture _____

mortuary _____

reflection _____

D THINKING CRITICALLY

1 Discussing the Story

Discuss the following questions with a partner, in a small group, or with the whole class:

1 Does Jackson tell us when (the year) and where (the town) the story takes place? Why?
2 Why does the village have a lottery?
3 Describe the character Tessie Hutchinson.
4 How does Tessie's husband react to her protests of unfairness? How do her neighbors react?
5 When do you first realize that something bad is going to happen? What words and images are omens of the future horror?
6 Why does the author choose stones as the weapons?

2 Making Inferences

> Authors often write something that is intended to have more than one meaning. While you read, look for meanings that are not explicitly stated – these are inferences. Making inferences will help you enjoy the reading on a different level. The story now has deeper significance, and you will have a better understanding of it.

Read the following lines from the story. Then circle the letter of the best inference.

1 The villagers kept their distance, leaving a space between themselves and the stool. . . . (lines 44–45)
   a The villagers don't care about the stool.
   b The villagers are afraid of the ritual symbolized by the stool.
   c The stool is not very special.

2 A sudden hush fell on the crowd as Mr. Summers cleared his throat and looked at the list. (lines 146–147)
   a The people take the lottery very seriously.
   b Mr. Summers likes to feel important.
   c The people in the village hope Mr. Summers will call their names.

3 "Used to be a saying about 'Lottery in June, corn be heavy soon.'" (lines 186–187)
   a The villagers need to have rain for their crops.
   b People are not superstitious.
   c The lottery is related to the harvest.

3 Analyzing the Story: Irony

Look back at the Literary Term on page 71. There are many examples of irony in this story when things do not turn out as we expect. Read the story again and find the examples below. Complete the chart with the reality (or the irony) for each. Then add your own example from the story. What is the expectation? What really happened?

EXAMPLE	EXPECTATION	REALITY (IRONY)
1 The morning of June 27th was clear and sunny, with the fresh warmth of a full-summer day; . . . The people of the village began to gather in the square. . . . (lines 1–4)	It's a pleasant day and the people are getting together for a holiday or a celebration.	
2 Bobby Martin had already stuffed his pockets full of stones . . . eventually made a great pile of stones in one corner of the square. . . . (lines 14–18)	He and the other boys are playing a game.	

3 Soon the women . . . began to call their children, and the children came reluctantly, having to be called four or five times. (lines 28–31)	The children don't understand that it is a special day and that they will have fun.		
4 (lines _____ – _____)			

Pair Discussion   With a partner, compare what you have written. Correct any mistakes you find. When do you begin to understand that the reality is very different from first appearance? How does this make you feel?

4 Writing

Read the writing ideas that follow. Your instructor may make specific assignments or ask you to choose one of these:

1 Many people feel that humans are inherently violent. How does this story illustrate the violent nature of people? Can we ever expect people to become nonviolent? Write an essay about these issues.

2 Write out the specific rules of the lottery according to the description in the story. Include all the details and the order in which the rules are administered. (You may work with a partner.)

3 Pretend you are a newspaper reporter covering the story of this town's lottery. Write an eyewitness account of what you observe.

4 Describe how one of Mrs. Hutchinson's children felt when his/her mother opened the piece of paper. Write the description in the first person.

5 Compare and contrast the use of atmosphere in "The Lottery" with another story in this book, such as "All Summer in a Day" by Ray Bradbury.

6 An *allegory* is defined as a story with characters and actions that symbolize ideas and morals. For example, in the fable "The Tortoise and the Hare" the tortoise symbolizes perseverance. Do you think "The Lottery" is an allegory? Write about what "The Lottery" could symbolize, using examples from the story.

CHAPTER 6

The One Day War

Judith Soloway

A PREPARING TO READ

1 Think Before You Read

Answer the following questions:

1 What do you know about the Civil War in the United States?
2 What is a bicentennial celebration?
3 Have you ever seen a military cemetery? Describe what you remember.
4 Read the first paragraph only and try to guess what the story is about.
5 How do you feel when you see films about wars or read about them? Have you ever been in a war?

2 Literary Term: Satire

Do you sometimes say the opposite of what you mean? We often use sarcasm to show our disapproval of an action, idea, or person. When writers want to show disapproval, they may use **satire** to emphasize a human failure, weakness, or vice. Satire can be gentle and humorous or bitter and savage. The situations, characters, and language of satire help create the tone of the story.

3 Idioms and Expressions

You will find these idioms and expressions in the story:

rolling along proceeding efficiently	**speak for** represent
fall into place work out well	**at a fraction of the cost** much less money
know well in advance know at a much earlier time	

B THE STORY

About the Author

Judith Soloway (born in 1950) was born in Brooklyn, New York. While attending Hunter College High School in Manhattan, she wrote for the school newspaper and considered a career in journalism. Instead, after graduating from Queens College, she became a teacher; she has taught English in Maryland, Pennsylvania, New York, and Florida. Soloway is married and has four daughters. She writes poetry and short stories in her spare time.

The inspiration for "The One Day War" came while Soloway was passing a large military cemetery during a motor trip. She was struck by the miles and miles of graves and their cold anonymity.

The One Day War

Good morning fellow Americans. Welcome to The One Day War. WCDW will be your eyes and ears for today bringing you live coverage of a momentous day in our history. As part of our bicentennial celebration of the Civil War, we are proud to participate in Professor
5   Brainard's project, The One Day War.

I'm sure there isn't an American out there who hasn't heard of the project. It has been the most talked about subject in our country for many months. Now the great day, April 9, 2065, is here, and we are all part of it.

10   The weather is perfect and visibility is excellent. There isn't a cloud overhead; the sky is blue and clear. From our place here on the grandstand, we have a perfect vantage point. While we are waiting, we've arranged an exclusive interview with Professor Brainard, father of The One Day War.

15   "Professor, I know how busy you are supervising this enormous undertaking, and we appreciate your giving us an interview. To begin with, could you give us some background information about the project?"

"I am very pleased to speak with you. At this point, the project is rolling along according to schedule, and I am here to advise on any
20   problems that may arise. You asked for some background. Well, as you may know, I'm considered an expert on the Civil War, and I was asked to plan a bicentennial celebration. One disturbing aspect of the Civil War, like any other war, was how expensive and inefficient it was. Using our modern day technology, we are able to reconstruct one battle that is the
25   equivalent of all the battles fought during the entire war!

"The major expenses in any war involve the movement of troops and machinery, medical equipment and personnel, and burial expenses. Doing all this during wartime is difficult, expensive, and inefficient. Given our cultural and scientific development these past two hundred
30   years, there was no reason we couldn't produce the same effect at a fraction of the cost. The most brilliant part of the plan was the most obvious – why not bury the soldiers right on the battlefield and eliminate a lot of cost and trouble. The battlefield becomes the cemetery! Once we settled on this idea, the other details fell into place.

35   "An assembly line procedure was adopted. The computer chose the soldiers. We hired digging crews, masons, gardeners, and florists. We saved a tremendous amount of money by not needing any war machinery except for one revolver per soldier. Naturally, there was no need for medical teams and supplies. The families of the soldiers knew well in
40   advance, so they could plan accordingly and put their personal affairs in order."

"Did you encounter any difficulties with the plan?"

"A little, at first. Some members of Congress thought the plan was 'inhumane.' I explained to them that the net result was the same as waging the war for four years at a greater expense and inconvenience to the general population. Moreover, there would be no involvement with civilians whatsoever – no attacks, no burning of houses, no families killed by marauding soldiers. They agreed unanimously that my plan was safer, more efficient, and more humane than the Civil War.

"We did encounter a strong objection from the Western Union lobby in Washington. They would be losing revenue from the telegrams usually sent to the families of the soldiers. We worked out an agreement allowing the company to manufacture the small American flags that will be given to each family."

"And now, Professor Brainard, after months of planning, your project is about to become a reality. Thank you, Professor. I know I speak for the entire nation when I salute you as a remarkable man and a true patriot."

It's 8:30, and we are almost ready for the project to get under way. Before us on this immense battlefield, stretched out for miles, are the two opposing armies. The soldiers stand at attention in neat rows – an army of blue facing an army of gray. They stand very still like marble statues. On our left, we can see the digging machines and their crews waiting silently. Behind them are the masons and gardeners. On our right, we can see the florists.

Here in the grandstand are all the dignitaries: the President, Vice President, Speaker of the House, Senate Majority Leader, members of the Cabinet, the Supreme Court Justices, and representatives of the Armed Forces.

We all rise for our National Anthem. The President approaches the podium. When he gives the signal, the band will play *Taps*, and on the last note of *Taps*, watch the soldiers.

With military precision, each man withdraws his pistol, places it to his temple, and in unison 204,000 shots ring out. The noise is deafening like a huge explosion. Gunsmoke fills the air. The sky is now gray as if a storm has suddenly blown in. The field is very quiet. The rows of gray and blue fallen bodies are now irregular. I guess it's hard to plan a perfect fall even with intensive training and devotion to one's country. The soldiers have done their part. Now it's time for the rest of the team to go to work.

The grandstand viewers file out of their seats and into the waiting limousines. The President shakes Professor Brainard's hand. As the last officials leave, the digging machines and their crews move onto the field. They work from left to right digging each trench, burying each body, and leveling the ground. The stone masons follow. They place a stone at each soldier's grave. Every stone has already been engraved

with the soldier's name and dates of birth and death. The crews work efficiently, row after row. The landscapers follow the masons. They place strips of sod over the newly dug earth. Now the florists unload their
90 trucks and put fresh floral bouquets on each grave.

We are watching the final phase of The One Day War. The digging crews have left the field, the masons have gone, the florists are leaving, and the buses of widows and orphans are arriving. All the families of the soldiers will be here at the same time. They have all been transported
95 here at government expense. They file out onto the field. The ushers and hostesses, dressed in tuxedos and long gowns, direct each family to its particular gravesite. Each family receives an identification tag and a small American flag. The military band is playing *When Johnny Comes Marching Home Again*. We all stand at attention as a gentle breeze blows
100 over the field.

It is truly amazing what American ingenuity can accomplish. This morning what was an ordinary field has been transformed into a military cemetery. It has been a beautiful day! I've been honored to help bring this momentous project into your homes. Yes, it's been a perfect day.
105 Good night, Americans. Sleep well.

C UNDERSTANDING THE STORY

1 Reading Comprehension

Answer these questions to determine how well you understood the story:

1 Where and when does this story take place?
2 Who is the narrator? To whom is he speaking?
3 Who is Professor Brainard? Why is he called a patriot?
4 Which people are on the grandstand?
5 What does *war machinery* mean?
6 What does an *assembly line procedure* mean? Why is it used?
7 Why do the grandstand viewers leave the scene of the battlefield?
8 Why are the families of the soldiers given American flags?

2 Guessing Meaning from Context

The words below are in the story. Find the words in the story and try to understand their meanings. Look at the four definitions for each word and circle the correct one.

1 momentous
- **a** soon
- **b** motherly
- **c** sudden
- **(d)** important

2 vantage point
- **a** pencil
- **b** control
- **c** viewing position
- **d** power point

3 mason
- **a** friend
- **b** dancer
- **c** enemy
- **d** stonecutter

4 revolver
- **a** door
- **b** car
- **c** gun
- **d** sun

5 marauding
- **a** controlled
- **b** kind
- **c** friendly
- **d** rampaging

6 revenue
- **a** income
- **b** meeting
- **c** memory
- **d** dream

7 podium
- **a** medicine
- **b** platform
- **c** vegetable
- **d** hatred

8 sod
- **a** earth with grass
- **b** flower
- **c** unhappy
- **d** talked

9 visibility
- **a** math function
- **b** hat
- **c** darkness
- **d** clarity of the air

10 temple

    a side of the forehead   **c** cheek

    b chin   **d** neck

11 unison

    a fictional animal   **c** happiness

    b only son   **d** at the same time

12 usher

    a winner   **c** escort

    b sleeper   **d** doctor

13 ingenuity

    a reality   **c** innocence

    b cleverness   **d** integrity

3 Grammar: Active and Passive Voice

Sentences are written in either the active or passive voice. In the active voice, the subject is doing the action.

Example:

"We **hired** digging crews, masons, gardeners, and florists."

In this sentence, the subject *we* did the hiring (performed the action). In the passive voice, the subject is acted upon. If we were to change the previous sentence to the passive voice, it would read like this:

The digging crews, masons, gardeners, and florists **were hired** by us.

Which sentence do you think is smoother? Obviously, the one in the active voice. It is generally better to write in the active voice because the active voice is more direct and stronger than the passive voice. If you use the passive voice excessively, it weakens your writing. However, there are times when the passive is preferred. For instance, the passive is generally used when the action is more important than the person doing the action.

Examples:
ACTIVE: The police **found** the lost child.
PASSIVE: The lost child **was found**. (The important fact is that the
  child was found. Who found the child is not as important.)
ACTIVE: Raul's mother **gave birth** to him in Chile.
PASSIVE: Raul **was born** in Chile.

The passive voice is formed by using the verb *to be* and a past
participle. The object of the verb in an active sentence becomes the
subject in a passive sentence; the subject from an active sentence
becomes the agent preceded by the preposition *by*. When you change
a verb from active to passive, make sure the new verb agrees with its
subject.

Examples:

        SUBJECT   VERB   OBJECT
ACTIVE: Many people watch the television program.

PASSIVE: The television program is watched by many people.
        SUBJECT   PASSIVE VERB   AGENT

It often sounds awkward to use the preposition *by* and the agent. If
this is the case, it may be better to leave them out of the sentence, as
shown here:

Examples:
AWKWARD: The skyscraper was built in 1924 by workers.
CORRECT: **The skyscraper was built in 1924.**

Application 1   Rewrite each active sentence as a passive sentence.

1 The coach praised the team.

   The team was praised by the coach.

2 The scientist supervised every aspect of the project.

3 They could produce the same effect more efficiently.

_____

4 We worked out an agreement with the company.

_____

5 We encountered a strong objection.

_____

6 They approved the plan unanimously.

_____

7 The soldiers heard the music.

_____

8 The reporter interviewed Dr. Brainard.

_____

9 The ushers led the families to the gravesites.

_____

Application 2   Rewrite each passive sentence in the active voice and then decide which sentence sounds better – the active or passive. Remember: When using the passive voice, you must use the past participle.

1 They were married in Las Vegas by a judge.

A judge in Las Vegas married them.

2 The buildings were destroyed in the earthquake.

_____

3 My brother was fired from his job.

_____

4 The ruins of the ancient city were found in the desert.

_____

5 His car was hit by a motorcycle.

_____

6 He was told to apply for a fellowship.

_____

4 Editing

A television reporter was the first journalist on the scene of an explosion. The following story is what she reported. Edit the story by changing the active voice to the passive.

An explosion has destroyed the building. It killed many people. The explosion injured many others. They are taking the injured to several hospitals in the area. They have brought doctors and nurses here. The Red Cross has requested blood donors to contact its offices. Police have blocked off the center of the city.

D THINKING CRITICALLY

1 Discussing the Story

Discuss the following questions with a partner, in a small group, or with the whole class:

1 At what point in the story do you realize what Brainard's project is really about?
2 According to Professor Brainard, what are some disturbing aspects of the Civil War?
3 Why is Brainard's plan efficient? Are there any faults in his plan? What are they?
4 How do you feel about the soldiers? Are they heroes?
5 How does the author feel about war?
6 The narrator states, "I guess it's hard to plan a perfect fall even with intensive training and devotion to one's country." Look for other examples of satire.

2 Making Inferences

> Authors often write something that is intended to have more than one meaning. While you read, look for meanings that are not explicitly stated – these are inferences. Making inferences will help you enjoy the reading on a different level. The story now has deeper significance, and you will have a better understanding of it.

Read the following lines from the story. Then circle the letter of the best inference.

1 One disturbing aspect of the Civil War, like any other war, was how expensive and inefficient it was. (lines 22–23)

a Expense and inefficiency are not the most disturbing aspects of war.

b War should not cost people a lot of money in taxes.

c Some people make a lot of money during wars.

2 It is truly amazing what American ingenuity can accomplish. (line 101)

a We are a very creative nation.

b We can accomplish anything when we put our minds to work.

c American ingenuity could have been put to better use.

3 Good night, Americans. Sleep well. (line 105)

a People accept the sacrifice of soldiers.

b Americans shouldn't be able to sleep well after so much death and destruction.

c Volunteer armies know the rules of war.

3 Analyzing the Story: Satire

Satire is a style of writing in which the author shows disapproval of something. Though the author does not state her point literally, we as readers sense it from her ironic and sarcastic tone. In "The One Day War," the subject is war and its cost in human lives. How does the author really feel about the subject?

In the chart below find the satirical language in the story. In your own words, write the point you think the author is trying to make.

LANGUAGE FROM THE STORY	AUTHOR'S POINT
1 One disturbing aspect of the Civil War . . . was how expensive and inefficient it was. (lines 22–23)	*The worst aspect of war is the waste of human life.*
2 Given our cultural and scientific development . . . no reason we couldn't produce the same effect at a fraction of the cost. (lines 29–31)	
3 The most brilliant part of the plan was the most obvious . . . The battlefield becomes the cemetery! (lines 31–33)	
4 Some members of Congress thought the plan was "inhumane." (lines 43–44)	
5 The rows of gray and blue fallen bodies are now irregular. I guess it's hard to plan a perfect fall even with intensive training. . . . (lines 76–78)	

Pair Discussion   With a partner, compare what you have written. Correct any mistakes you find. Can you add any more examples of satire from the story? What point is the author making in each?

4 Writing

Read the writing ideas that follow. Your instructor may make specific assignments or ask you to choose one of these:

1 Prepare to interview someone who survived a war. List some questions you would ask.
2 Pretend you are the president of the United States in 2065. Write a speech you would deliver to the nation on the day of Brainard's project.
3 Write a letter to the family of one of the soldiers who died.
4 Create a dialogue between the wife and child of a dead soldier.
5 Notice the contrast between the beautiful, clear weather and the purpose of the day. Does this contrast add to the irony of the story? What other words and images help create irony? Write about the irony in the story.
6 What are your own feelings about war? Are wars necessary? Write an essay about your views.

TAKE A CLOSER LOOK

1 Analyzing and Comparing

In each of the following sections, you are asked to think about and compare two of the stories in Part Two.

"The Last Leaf " and "The Lottery"

- Both of these stories deal with sacrifice. How are the sacrifices similar? How are they different?
- Is Mrs. Hutchinson a heroine? Is the painter a hero?
- Contrast the way each of these characters faces death.

"The Lottery" and "The One Day War"

- Compare the descriptions of the scenery in each story. How are they similar?
- Compare the way victims are chosen in both stories. Which method is more civilized? Defend your answer.
- Compare the physical descriptions of the settings in both stories.
- Select examples of irony from each story.

All Three Stories

- Compare the descriptions of the scenery in each story. How are they different?
- Select several examples of irony in each story.
- Which character do you sympathize with and why?

2 Freewriting

Fate is a theme in each of the stories in Part Two. For fifteen minutes, write about fate as it is treated in each of the stories. Could the characters escape their fates? If they could, how would the stories change? Have a character from one story give advice to a character in another story.

When you have finished writing, exchange papers with a classmate and discuss your reactions.

B WORDS FREQUENTLY CONFUSED

Words that have similar spellings, meanings, or pronunciations are often confused with one another. In the following exercise, you will use some of the words that appear in the stories in Part Two. For each section, choose the correct words and insert them in the sentences. Use your dictionary if you need help.

From "The Last Leaf"

statue (noun), statute (noun), stature (noun)

loose (adjective), lose (verb)

except (preposition), accept (verb)

light (verb), lit (verb)

leave (verb), live (verb), life (noun)

bored (verb), board (noun), boring (adjective)

1 She was very _____ by the _____ lecture.

2 We admired the _____ of Michelangelo's David.

3 The senators passed the _____ on the first vote.

4 The politician had lost his _____ in the community after the scandal.

5 He sawed the _____ into two pieces.

6 Put your keys in your pocket if you don't want to _____ them.

7 She likes to wear _____ clothes.

8 Did you _____ the fire in the fireplace?

9 Yes, I _____ the fire.

10 The teacher asked Leon to _____ the room.

11 Do you _____ with your family?

12 His grandfather lived a long _____.

13 I _____ your invitation and look forward to the party.

14 _____ for the bad weather, we had a wonderful vacation.

From "The Lottery"

precede (verb), proceed (verb)

rite (noun), right (adjective or noun), write (verb)

lead (noun or verb), led (verb)

draw (verb), drawer (noun)

1 Little children like to _____ with crayons.

2 The _____ in this antique desk is stuck.

3 Monday will always _____ Tuesday.

4 The judge said, "Shall we _____ with the hearing?"

5 "You can _____ a horse to water, but you cannot make it drink."

6 The conductor _____ the orchestra with great feeling.

7 The _____ in some paint can cause poisoning.

8 The word *ritual* is derived from the word _____.

9 The witness raised her _____ hand and swore to tell the truth.

10 It is a big accomplishment for a five-year-old child to _____ his or her name.

From "The One Day War"

rise (verb), raise (noun or verb)

human (noun), humane (adjective)

signal (noun or verb), sign (noun)

personal (adjective), personnel (noun)

noisy (adjective), nosey (adjective)

adopt (verb), adapt (verb), adept (adjective)

stripe (noun), striped (adjective), strip (noun), stripped (verb)

1 Antonio learned to _____ to his new school.

2 The young couple hoped to _____ a baby.

3 The sculptor was very _____ at working in stone.

4 What time do you _____ in the morning?

5 Did you _____ the shades to let in the sun?

6 I asked my boss for a(n) _____.

7 We hung the Welcome Home _____ over the door.

8 They could barely hear the S.O.S. _____ from the sinking ship.

9 The highway crew painted a yellow _____ on the road.

10 You should seal the package with a(n) _____ of tape.

11 She wore _____ pants and a red shirt.

12 The soldier was _____ of all his medals after he deserted his post.

13 The _____ children at the next table disturbed our dinner.

14 Our _____ neighbor likes to gossip about everyone on the street.

15 We belong to the _____ race, but we are not always _____.

16 We had a(n) _____ interest in the project.

17 When you interview for a job, you meet with someone in _____.

C SPELLING

Forming Noun Plurals and Past Tense Verbs

In Shirley Jackson's story, some *families* actually *enjoyed* the horrible custom of drawing names for the annual lottery. Notice that we change the *y* in *family* to an *i*, and then we add *-es* to pluralize the noun. With the verb *enjoy*, however, we form the past tense by keeping the *y* and adding *-ed*. Note the following rules for words ending in *y*:

1 If the *y* is preceded by a consonant, as in the noun *family*, we change the *y* to *i* and add *-es* to form the plural. The same is true for forming the past tense of verbs. *Study*, for example, becomes *studied* because the *y* is preceded by the consonant *d*. Here are some other examples:

NOUN SINGULAR/PLURAL	VERB PRESENT/PAST TENSE
victory victories	**try** tried
ally allies	**reply** replied
fly flies	**lie** lied

2 If, however, the *y* is preceded by a vowel, we just add the suffix *-s* for a noun and *-ed* for a verb. Note these examples:

NOUN SINGULAR/PLURAL	VERB PRESENT/PAST TENSE
day days	**employ** emloyed
valley valleys	**pray** prayed
toy toys	**play** played

For this exercise, form the plurals of the following nouns:

inquiry _____   history _____

baby _____   boy _____

community _____   alley _____

company _____   jury _____

bay _____   bunny _____

Now form the past tense of these verbs:

comply _____   hurry _____

worry _____   destroy _____

supply _____   busy _____

annoy _____   apply _____

D REVIEW TEST

1 Roots, Prefixes, and Suffixes

Match the prefixes and roots in the left-hand column with the definitions on the right. Write the number of the correct definition in the space provided.

____	micro	**1** study	**8** within		
____	mal	**2** love of	**9** small		
____	pre	**3** not	**10** before		
____	log	**4** earth	**11** bad		
____	phil	**5** head	**12** both		
____	ambi	**6** large	**13** against		
____	intra	**7** lead			
____	anti				
____	geo				
____	capi				

By studying the structure of the following words (their roots, prefixes, or suffixes), can you figure out their meanings? Write a definition or a synonym next to each word.

1 precede _____

2 transport _____

3 manuscript _____

4 biography _____

5 malnutrition _____

6 detach _____

7 antisocial _____

8 ambivalent _____

9 substandard _____

10 illiterate _____

2 Infinitives and Gerunds

Underline the correct infinitive or gerund in each of the following word combinations.

1 refuse (to come, coming)
2 want (to meet, meeting)
3 dislike (to take, taking)
4 decide (to buy, buying)
5 hope (to see, seeing)
6 try (to find, finding)
7 keep (to read, reading)
8 seems (to be, being)
9 delay (to write, writing)
10 avoid (to travel, traveling)

3 Active and Passive Voice

In each of the following sentences, the verb is in either the active or passive voice. Underline the verb, and in the space provided to the right of each sentence, write *A* for active voice or *P* for passive voice.

1 The game was won by the Yankees's star pitcher. ____

2 The American Civil War was fought by the North and the South. ____

3 A lottery was held each year by the villagers. ____

4 Tess Hutchinson drew the paper with the black spot. ____

5 In the One Day War, 204,000 soldiers killed themselves with their own pistols. ____

6 Mr. Behrman painted a leaf on a wall to save a young woman's life. ____

7 Many artists live in Greenwich Village. ____

8 The names of the families participating in the lottery were read by Mr. Summers. ____

Now rewrite all of the sentences that are in the passive voice, putting them into the active voice.

 WEBQUEST

Find more information about the topics in Part Two by going on the Internet. Go to www.cambridge.org/discoveringfiction/wq and follow the instructions for doing a WebQuest. Have fun. Enjoy the quest!

PART THREE

Irony

IRONY, WHICH is sometimes defined as "a cruel twist of fate," is a technique used by many famous authors. Perhaps that is because in real life we're always running into ironic situations that make us realize how much our existence is governed by chance or luck. You have already encountered some ironic elements in Part Two.

Not all irony has to be tragic, however. You will be amused by the turn of events in "The Third Level," the first story in this part of the book.

CHAPTER 7

The Third Level

JACK FINNEY

 PREPARING TO READ

1 Think Before You Read

Answer the following questions before you read the story:

1 If it were possible to travel back in time, what place and time in history would you choose?
2 Many people think that life was simpler a hundred years ago. Do you agree or disagree?
3 The following words refer to fashion styles in the 1890s. Try to find pictures of these styles in a dictionary or encyclopedia.

derby hat   high-buttoned shoes
leg-of-mutton sleeves   sideburns
handlebar mustache   sleeve protectors

2 Literary Term: Romanticism

The romantic movement in art, literature, and music began in the early nineteenth century in Europe. **Romanticism** reflects the writer's interest in nature and sentimental feelings about life. When we romanticize someone or something, we concentrate on all the good qualities and forget the negatives. Romanticism involves seeing life as we would like it to be, while looking at the world through rose-colored glasses.

3 Idioms and Expressions

You will find these idioms and expressions in the story:

skin me cheat me, trick me out of money	**didn't pass a soul** didn't see anyone
ducked into bent one's head down to enter	**drew three hundred dollars out** took three hundred dollars out of a bank account
got lost couldn't find the way out	

B THE STORY

About the Author

Jack Finney (1911–1995), a well-known novelist and short-story writer whose theme is usually traveling through time, was born in Milwaukee, Wisconsin. Finney lived in New York City for a while, working as an advertising copywriter and writing suspense stories for various magazines.

In 1954 he published his first novel, *Five against the House*, which details the plot of a group of college students to rob a casino in Reno, Nevada. The next year Finney published *The Body Snatchers*, which inspired the film *The Invasion of the Body Snatchers*. His most famous novel, *Time and Again*, was published in 1970; it is about an advertising artist who manages to break the time barrier and send himself to New York City in the 1880s.

You will find this same theme in "The Third Level," in which a commuter discovers a train that travels to the year 1894. You may also want to read Finney's sequel, *From Time to Time*, published in 1995, in which the main character travels back to the year 1912 in hopes of preventing the sinking of the *Titanic*.

The Third Level

The presidents of the New York Central and the New York, New Haven and Hartford railroads will swear on a stack of timetables that there are only two. But I say there are three, because I've *been* on the third level at Grand Central Station. Yes, I've taken the obvious step: I talked
5 to a psychiatrist friend of mine, among others. I told him about the third level at Grand Central Station, and he said it was a waking-dream wish fulfillment. He said I was unhappy. That made my wife kind of mad, but he explained that he meant the modern world is full of insecurity, fear, war, worry and all the rest of it, and that I just want to escape. Well,
10 who doesn't? Everybody I know wants to escape, but they don't wander down into any third level at Grand Central Station.

But that's the reason, he said, and my friends all agreed. Everything points to it, they claimed. My stamp collecting, for example; that's a "temporary refuge from reality." Well, maybe, but my grandfather didn't
15 need any refuge from reality; things were pretty nice and peaceful in his day, from all I hear, and he started my collection. It's a nice collection, too, blocks of four of practically every U.S. issue, first-day covers, and so on. President Roosevelt collected stamps, too, you know.

Anyway, here's what happened at Grand Central. One night last
20 summer I worked late at the office. I was in a hurry to get uptown to my apartment so I decided to take the subway from Grand Central because it's faster than the bus.

Now, I don't know why this should have happened to me. I'm just an ordinary guy named Charley, thirty-one years old, and I was wearing
25 a tan gabardine suit and a straw hat with a fancy band; I passed a dozen men who looked just like me. And I wasn't trying to escape from anything; I just wanted to get home to Louisa, my wife.

I turned into Grand Central from Vanderbilt Avenue, and went down the steps to the first level, where you take trains like the Twentieth
30 Century. Then I walked down another flight to the second level, where the suburban trains leave from, ducked into an arched doorway heading

for the subway – and got lost. That's easy to do. I've been in and out of Grand Central hundreds of times, but I'm always bumping into new doorways and stairs and corridors. Once I got into a tunnel about a mile long and came out in the lobby of the Roosevelt Hotel. Another time I came up in an office building on Forty-sixth Street, three blocks away.

Sometimes I think Grand Central is growing like a tree, pushing out new corridors and staircases like roots. There's probably a long tunnel that nobody knows about feeling its way under the city right now, on its way to Times Square, and maybe another to Central Park. And maybe – because for so many people through the years Grand Central *has* been an exit, a way of escape – maybe that's how the tunnel I got into . . . But I never told my psychiatrist friend about that idea.

The corridor I was in began angling left and slanting downward and I thought that was wrong, but I kept on walking. All I could hear was the empty sound of my own footsteps, and I didn't pass a soul. Then I heard that sort of hollow roar ahead that means open space and people talking. The tunnel turned sharp left; I went down a short flight of stairs and came out on the third level at Grand Central Station. For just a moment I thought I was back on the second level, but I saw the room was smaller, there were fewer ticket windows and train gates, and the information booth in the center was wood and old-looking. And the man in the booth wore a green eyeshade and long black sleeve protectors. The lights were dim and sort of flickering. Then I saw why; they were open-flame gaslights.

There were brass spittoons on the floor, and across the station a glint of light caught my eye; a man was pulling a gold watch from his vest pocket. He snapped open the cover, glanced at his watch, and frowned. He wore a derby hat, a black four-button suit with tiny lapels, and he had a big, black, handlebar mustache. Then I looked around and saw that everyone in the station was dressed like eighteen-ninety- something; I never saw so many beards, sideburns, and fancy mustaches in my life. A woman walked in through the train gate; she wore a dress with leg-of-mutton sleeves and skirts to the top of her high-buttoned shoes. Back of her, out on the tracks, I caught a glimpse of a locomotive, a very small Currier & Ives locomotive with a funnel-shaped stack. And then I knew.

To make sure, I walked over to a newsboy and glanced at the stack of papers at his feet. It was *The World*; and *The World* hasn't been published for years. The lead story said something about President Cleveland. I've found that front page since, in the Public Library files, and it was printed June 11, 1894.

I turned toward the ticket windows knowing that here – on the third level at Grand Central – I could buy tickets that would take Louisa and me anywhere in the United States we wanted to go. In the year 1894. And I wanted two tickets to Galesburg, Illinois.

Have you ever been there? It's a wonderful town still, with big old frame houses, huge lawns, and tremendous trees whose branches meet overhead and roof the streets. And in 1894, summer evenings were twice as long, and people sat out on their lawns, the men smoking cigars and talking quietly, the women waving palm-leaf fans, with the fireflies all around, in a peaceful world. To be back there with the First World War still twenty years off, and World War II, over forty years in the future . . . I wanted two tickets for that.

The clerk figured the fare – he glanced at my fancy hatband, but he figured the fare – and I had enough for two coach tickets, one way. But when I counted out the money and looked up, the clerk was staring at me. He nodded at the bills. "That ain't money, mister," he said, "and if you're trying to skin me you won't get very far," and he glanced at the cash drawer beside him. Of course the money in his drawer was old-style bills, half again as big as the money we use nowadays, and different-looking. I turned away and got out fast. There's nothing nice about jail, even in 1894.

And that was that. I left the same way I came, I suppose. Next day, during lunch hour, I drew three hundred dollars out of the bank, nearly all we had, and bought old-style currency (that *really* worried my psychiatrist friend). You can buy old money at almost any coin dealer's, but you have to pay a premium. My three hundred dollars bought less than two hundred in old-style bills, but I didn't care; eggs were thirteen cents a dozen in 1894.

But I've never again found the corridor that leads to the third level at Grand Central Station, although I've tried often enough.

Louisa was pretty worried when I told her all this, and didn't want me to look for the third level any more, and after a while I stopped; I went back to my stamps. But now we're *both* looking, every weekend, because now we have proof that the third level is still there. My friend Sam Weiner disappeared! Nobody knew where, but I sort of suspected because Sam's a city boy, and I used to tell him about Galesburg – I went to school there – and he always said he liked the sound of the place. And that's where he is, all right. In 1894.

Because one night, fussing with my stamp collection, I found – well, do you know what a first-day cover is? When a new stamp is issued, stamp collectors buy some and use them to mail envelopes to themselves on the very first day of sale; and the postmark proves the date. The envelope is called a first-day cover. They're never opened; you just put blank paper in the envelope.

That night, among my oldest first-day covers, I found one that shouldn't have been there. But there it was. It was there because someone had mailed it to my grandfather at his home in Galesburg; that's what the address on the envelope said. And it had been there since July 18,

120 1894 – the postmark showed that – yet I didn't remember it at all. The stamp was a six-cent, dull brown, with a picture of President Garfield. Naturally, when the envelope came to Granddad in the mail, it went right into his collection and stayed there – till I took it out and opened it.

The paper inside wasn't blank. It read:

125
                                        941 Willard Street
                                        Galesburg, Illinois
                                        July 18, 1894

Charley:

I got to wishing that you were right. Then I got to believing you
130 were right. And, Charley, it's true; I found the third level! I've been here two weeks, and right now, down the street at the Dalys', someone is playing a piano, and they're all out on the front porch singing, "Seeing Nellie Home." And I'm invited over for lemonade. Come on back, Charley and Louisa. Keep looking till you find the third level! It's
135 worth it, believe me!

The note is signed *Sam*.

At the stamp and coin store I go to, I found out that Sam bought eight hundred dollars' worth of old-style currency. That ought to set him up
140 in a nice little hay, feed and grain business; he always said that's what he really wished he could do, and he certainly can't go back to his old business. Not in Galesburg, Illinois, in 1894. His old business? Why, Sam was my psychiatrist.

C UNDERSTANDING THE STORY

1 Reading Comprehension

Answer these questions to determine how well you understood the story:

1 In what city does most of the story take place? How do you know?
2 Who is the narrator?
3 Where is the third level?
4 What is Charley's hobby?
5 How does Charley know he has gone back in time? Give some specific details from the story.
6 What is the date on the newspaper *The World*?
7 What tickets does Charley want to buy? Why?
8 Who sent Charley a letter, and where was the letter from?

2 Guessing Meaning from Context

Read each of the following sentences. The words in bold are in the story.
Find the words in the story and try to understand their meanings. Write a
synonym for each word next to the sentence.

1 Yes, I've taken the **obvious** step. (line 4) _____ *logical* _____

2 Everything points to it, they **claimed**. My stamp collecting . . . that's a
   "temporary **refuge** from reality." (lines 12–14) _____

   _____

3 I was wearing a tan **gabardine** suit. (lines 24–25) _____

4 I'm always **bumping** into new doorways and stairs and **corridors**.
   (lines 33–34) _____   _____

5 The corridor I was in began **angling** left and **slanting** downward.
   (line 44) _____   _____

6 I heard that sort of **hollow** roar. (lines 46–47) _____

7 I went down a short **flight** of stairs. (lines 48–49) _____

8 The lights were dim and sort of **flickering**. (line 54) _____

9 I walked over to a newsboy and **glanced** at the stack of papers at his feet.
   (lines 67–68) _____

10 You can buy old money . . . but you have to pay a **premium**.
   (lines 96–97) _____

Some of the words you have just defined can have alternate meanings.
Look at these same words in the following sentences. Insert the appropriate
synonyms, according to the way the words are used here.

1 It was **obvious** that Bob did not know the answer to the question.

   _____ *apparent* _____

2 In 1849, when miners found gold in Alaska, they immediately staked a **claim**. _____

3 When I fell down, I got a **bump** on my head. _____

4 Maria is always **angling** to get special favors. _____

5 A good reporter must never **slant** the news. _____

6 After his sickness, his face had a **hollow** look. _____

7 Our **flight** to North Carolina was a short one. _____

8 The bullet just **glanced** off the policeman's shoulder. It didn't hurt him. _____

9 I must pay the **premium** on my insurance policy. _____

3 Grammar: Reflexive and Intensive Pronouns

In Jack Finney's story, the main character, Charley, discovers the third level by *himself*. What kind of pronoun is *himself*? It is called a reflexive pronoun because the word reflects back to the subject. For example, if you fell down and hurt your knee, you would say, "I hurt **myself**." Or, if you were trying to control a mischievous child, you might command, "Behave **yourself**."

Like other personal pronouns, the *self* words have both singular and plural forms. The singular pronouns are: *myself, yourself, himself, herself, oneself,* and *itself*.

You may also use a *self* pronoun for emphasis. These pronouns are called intensive pronouns, and they are written exactly the same as the reflexive pronouns. If Charley's wife didn't believe his story about the third level, he would insist, "I **myself** saw it." Note that this *self* pronoun immediately follows the subject.

Examples:
You **yourself** invited them.
He **himself** made the call.

continued

We often use the *self* pronouns after the prepositions *by, to,* and *for*.

Examples:
She lives **by herself**. (She lives alone.)
He always sits **by himself** in class. (He sits away from others.)
Mary often talks **to herself** in class. (She is not talking to others.)
Tom made dinner **for himself**. (Tom prepared his own dinner.)

Note: With certain verbs you may **not** use a *self* pronoun. These verbs are: *feel, relax,* and *concentrate*.

Examples:
I feel tired today. (*Not:* I feel myself tired.)
I can't concentrate with that loud music. (*Not:* I can't concentrate myself.)
Tom should relax. (*Not:* Tom should relax himself.)

Another important rule to remember: **Never** use the *self* pronouns as part of a compound subject.

Examples:
INCORRECT: Charley and himself searched for the third level.
CORRECT: **Charley and he** searched for the third level.
INCORRECT: My friend and myself saw a great movie last night.
CORRECT: **My friend and I** saw a great movie last night.

Likewise, do **not** use a *self* pronoun as part of a compound object.

Examples:
INCORRECT: Charley never told Sam or themselves his secret.
CORRECT: Charley never told **Sam or them** his secret.
INCORRECT: Susan helped Frank and myself.
CORRECT: Susan helped **Frank and me**.

Be careful not to confuse the *self* pronouns with the expression *each other*. Can you tell the difference in meaning between these two sentences?

Charley and Louise talk to themselves.
Charley and Louise talk to each other.

In the first sentence, both Charley and Louise speak aloud to themselves. In the second sentence, they communicate with each other; they carry on a conversation.

Application   In each of the following sentences, use a *self* pronoun or the expression *each other*.

1 Lonely people often talk to _____*themselves*_____.

2 Charley and Sam never told _____ how to reach the third level.

3 Charley promised _____ that he would find the third level again.

4 In "A Day's Wait," Schatz and his father did not discuss with _____ the child's fear.

5 Johnsy told _____ that she would die when the last leaf fell from the vine.

6 You must not expect the government to help you. You must help _____.

7 Vicky and her mother never talked to _____ about serious matters.

8 Mrs. Jones lived by _____.

4 Editing

Underline and correct any errors you find in the following paragraph:

My friend, Nora and myself, have always been interested in stories about traveling through time. We found out for each other many authors who have used this theme in their work. Nora says that reading such stories helps her relax herself, and even when she is nervous, she can concentrate herself on the plot. For her birthday Nora bought some books by Jack Finney for herself. She also gave his novel to her sister and myself. This novel, *Time and Again*, is the kind of book my friend and myself can read aloud to ourselves when we get together.

THINKING CRITICALLY

1 Discussing the Story

Discuss the following questions with a partner, in a small group, or with the whole class:

1 What was life like in Galesburg, Illinois, in 1894?
2 Why do you think Charley has a desire to escape reality?
3 Why does Charley like to collect stamps?
4 Describe Charley's relationship with his wife Louisa.
5 Why does Charley tell Sam about the third level?
6 Why does Sam go to Galesburg?

2 Making Inferences

> Authors often write something that is intended to have more than one meaning. While you read, look for meanings that are not explicitly stated – these are inferences. Making inferences will help you enjoy the reading on a different level. The story now has deeper significance, and you will have a better understanding of it.

Read the following lines from the story. What can you infer about character, setting, plot, or theme? Write your answer on the line below.

1 I told him (a psychiatrist) about the third level . . . and he said it was a waking dream wish fulfillment. (lines 5–7)

   The psychiatrist didn't believe the third level existed in reality.

2 I passed a dozen men who looked just like me. (lines 25–26)

   _____

3 All I could hear was the empty sound of my own footsteps and I didn't pass a soul. (lines 45–46)

   _____

4 And in 1894, summer evenings were twice as long, and people sat out on their lawns. . . . (lines 78–79)

_____

5 Keep looking till you find the third level! It's worth it. . . . (lines 134–135)

_____

3 Analyzing the Story: Romanticism

Look back at the Literary Term on page 111. In this story, the main character romanticizes life in the past. Read the story again and find all the elements of living in a past time that he finds appealing. Write them on the stairway. An example has been done for you.

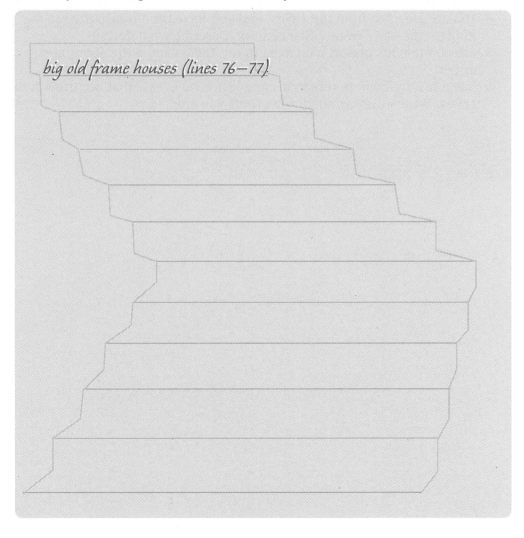

big old frame houses (lines 76–77)

Pair Discussion   With a partner, compare what you have written. Correct any mistakes you find. Draw a stairway with a time you would like to go back to. Write the elements of this past time that appeal to you on your stairway. Show your partner your stairway.

4 Writing

Read the writing ideas that follow. Your instructor may make specific assignments or ask you to choose one of these:

1 Imagine that Charley and his wife finally arrive in Galesburg, Illinois, in 1894. Write a dialogue between Charley and Sam when they meet.
2 Louisa decides that she doesn't like Galesburg and wants to return to New York. Continue the story.
3 Pretend that you have found the third level at Grand Central Station. To what place will you buy a ticket? Describe the place and your feelings when you arrive.
4 You are a person from the 1890s, and you have been transported to the future – the early twenty-first century. Describe what you see.
5 Select a famous person who lived in the 1890s, and write about him or her.
6 Use a history book to research some historical events that occurred in the 1890s. Write an essay about the events you studied.

CHAPTER 8

All Summer in a Day

RAY BRADBURY

A PREPARING TO READ

1 Think Before You Read

Answer the following questions before you read the story:

1 Read the beginning of the story, which describes the atmosphere or setting. Make a list of the sound and sight images. What specific words do you like?
2 Have you ever visited a rain forest or seen a tropical rain forest in a zoo? Describe what you saw.
3 How does weather affect our personalities?
4 What kind of climate do you prefer to live in?

2 Literary Term: Atmosphere

An author creates a physical setting for a story as well as the characters that move the plot along. The setting or **atmosphere** may have a tremendous impact on the story. In fact, the entire story may depend on this atmosphere.

3 Idioms and Expressions

You will find these idioms and expressions in the story:

get away move away	**muffled cries** sounds that are covered or blocked; hard to hear
let out allowed to go free	**gone wrong** changed unexpectedly
in a flash quickly	
whitened away the color faded	**meet each other's glances** look at each other

B THE STORY

About the Author

Ray Bradbury (born in 1920), born in Waukegan, Illinois, has traveled to distant galaxies and to the future in many of his stories. He is referred to as a science fiction writer or fantasist. His characters are not always realistic, but they are human. His plots may be impossible, but we believe them.

As a child, Bradbury loved libraries and regarded books as an indispensable part of his life. The idea of book burning was loathsome to him and became a theme in many of his writings. In *Fahrenheit 451*, which was later made into a movie, books are burned in a futuristic totalitarian society. In real life, Bradbury had actual examples of repression and censorship, such as Nazi Germany, the blacklists of the McCarthy era, and the communist regimes. On a personal level, Bradbury's great-grandmother, ten times removed, had been accused and acquitted of being a witch during the Salem witch trials.

Bradbury began writing on a typewriter that he rented for ten cents a half hour. Perhaps this accounts for his brisk writing style. His writing is poetic and symbolic and leans toward the macabre. Though he began his career by writing for magazines, he has also written for television, theater, and Hollywood. He has even hosted a television show of his dramatized stories.

All Summer in a Day

"Ready?"

"Ready."

"Now?"

"Soon."

5   "Do the scientists really know? Will it happen today, will it?"

"Look, look; see for yourself!"

The children pressed to each other like so many roses, so many weeds, intermixed, peering out for a look at the hidden sun.

It rained.

10   It had been raining for seven years; thousands upon thousands of days compounded and filled from one end to the other with rain, with the drum and gush of water, with the sweet crystal fall of showers and the concussion of storms so heavy they were tidal waves come over the islands. A thousand forests had been crushed under the rain and grown

15   up a thousand times to be crushed again. And this was the way life was forever on the planet Venus, and this was the schoolroom of the children of the rocket men and women who had come to a raining world to set up civilization and live out their lives.

"It's stopping, it's stopping!"

20   "Yes, yes!"

Margot stood apart from them, from these children who could never remember a time when there wasn't rain and rain and rain. They were all nine years old, and if there had been a day, seven years ago, when the sun came out for an hour and showed its face to the stunned world,

25   they could not recall. Sometimes, at night, she heard them stir, in remembrance, and she knew they were dreaming and remembering gold or a yellow crayon or a coin large enough to buy the world with. She knew they thought they remembered a warmness, like a blushing in the face, in the body, in the arms and legs and trembling hands. But then

30   they always awoke to the tatting drum, the endless shaking down of clear bead necklaces upon the roof, the walk, the gardens, the forests, and their dreams were gone.

All day yesterday they had read in class about the sun. About how like a lemon it was, and how hot. And they had written small stories or
35   essays or poems about it:

I think the sun is a flower,
That blooms for just one hour.

40   That was Margot's poem, read in a quiet voice in the still classroom while the rain was falling outside.

"Aw, you didn't write that!" protested one of the boys.

"I did," said Margot. "I *did.*"

"William!" said the teacher.
45   But that was yesterday. Now the rain was slackening, and the children were crushed in the great thick windows.

"Where's teacher?"

"She'll be back."

"She'd better hurry, we'll miss it!"
50   They turned on themselves, like a feverish wheel, all tumbling spokes.

Margot stood alone. She was a very frail girl who looked as if she had been lost in the rain for years and the rain had washed out the blue from her eyes and the red from her mouth and the yellow from her hair. She was an old photograph dusted from an album, whitened away, and
55   if she spoke at all her voice would be a ghost. Now she stood, separate, staring at the rain and the loud wet world beyond the huge glass.

"What're *you* looking at?" said William.

Margot said nothing.

"Speak when you're spoken to." He gave her a shove. But she did
60   not move; rather she let herself be moved only by him and nothing else.

They edged away from her, they would not look at her. She felt them go away. And this was because she would play no games with them in the echoing tunnels of the underground city. If they tagged her and ran, she stood blinking after them and did not follow. When the class sang
65   songs about happiness and life and games her lips barely moved. Only when they sang about the sun and the summer did her lips move as she watched the drenched windows.

And then, of course, the biggest crime of all was that she had come here only five years ago from Earth, and she remembered the sun and
70   the way the sun was and the sky was when she was four in Ohio. And they, they had been on Venus all their lives, and they had been only two years old when last the sun came out and had long since forgotten the color and heat of it and the way it really was. But Margot remembered.

"It's like a penny," she said once, eyes closed.

"No, it's not!" the children cried.

"It's like a fire," she said, "in the stove."

"You're lying, you don't remember!" cried the children.

But she remembered and stood quietly apart from all of them and watched the patterning windows. And once, a month ago, she had refused to shower in the school shower rooms, had clutched her hands to her ears and over her head, screaming the water mustn't touch her head. So after that, dimly, dimly, she sensed it, she was different and they knew her difference and kept away.

There was talk that her father and mother were taking her back to Earth next year; it seemed vital to her that they do so, though it would mean the loss of thousands of dollars to her family. And so, the children hated her for all these reasons of big and little consequence. They hated her pale snow face, her waiting silence, her thinness, and her possible future.

"Get away!" The boy gave her another push. "What're you waiting for?"

Then, for the first time, she turned and looked at him. And what she was waiting for was in her eyes.

"Well, don't wait around here!" cried the boy savagely. "You won't see nothing!"

Her lips moved.

"Nothing!" he cried. "It was all a joke, wasn't it?" He turned to the other children. "Nothing's happening today. *Is* it?"

They all blinked at him and then, understanding, laughed and shook their heads. "Nothing, nothing!"

"Oh, but," Margot whispered, her eyes helpless. "But this is the day, the scientists predict, they say, they *know*, the sun . . ."

"All a joke!" said the boy, and seized her roughly. "Hey, everyone, let's put her in a closet before teacher comes!"

"No," said Margot, falling back.

They surged about her, caught her up and bore her, protesting, and then pleading, and then crying, back into a tunnel, a room, a closet, where they slammed and locked the door. They stood looking at the door and saw it tremble from her beating and throwing herself against it. They heard her muffled cries. Then, smiling, they turned and went out and back down the tunnel, just as the teacher arrived.

"Ready, children?" She glanced at her watch.

"Yes!" said everyone.

"Are we all here?"

"Yes!"

The rain slackened still more.

They crowded to the huge door.

The rain stopped.

It was as if, in the midst of a film concerning an avalanche, a tornado, a hurricane, a volcanic eruption, something had, first, gone wrong with the sound apparatus, thus muffling and finally cutting off all noise, all of the blasts and repercussions and thunders, and then, second, ripped the film from the projector and inserted in its place a peaceful tropical slide which did not move or tremor. The world ground to a standstill. The silence was so immense and unbelievable that you felt your ears had been stuffed or you had lost your hearing altogether. The children put their hands to their ears. They stood apart. The door slid back and the smell of the silent, waiting world came in to them.

The sun came out.

It was the color of flaming bronze and it was very large. And the sky around it was a blazing blue tile color. And the jungle burned with sunlight as the children, released from their spell, rushed out, yelling, into the springtime.

"Now, don't go too far," called the teacher after them. "You've only two hours, you know. You wouldn't want to get caught out!"

But they were running and turning their faces up to the sky and feeling the sun on their cheeks like a warm iron; they were taking off their jackets and letting the sun burn their arms.

"Oh, it's better than the sun lamps, isn't it?"

"Much, much better!"

They stopped running and stood in the great jungle that covered Venus, that grew and never stopped growing, tumultuously, even as you watched it. It was a nest of octopi, clustering up great arms of fleshlike weed, wavering, flowering in this brief spring. It was the color of rubber and ash, this jungle, from the many years without sun. It was the color of stones and white cheeses and ink, and it was the color of the moon.

The children lay out, laughing, on the jungle mattress, and heard it sigh and squeak under them, resilient and alive. They ran among the trees, they slipped and fell, they pushed each other, they played hide-and-seek and tag, but most of all they squinted at the sun until tears ran down their faces, they put their hands up to that yellowness and that amazing blueness and they breathed of the fresh, fresh air and listened and listened to the silence which suspended them in a blessed sea of no sound and no motion. They looked at everything and savored everything. Then, wildly, like animals escaped from their caves, they ran and ran in shouting circles. They ran for an hour and did not stop running.

And then –

In the midst of their running one of the girls wailed.

Everyone stopped.

The girl, standing in the open, held out her hand.

"Oh, look, look," she said, trembling.

They came slowly to look at her opened palm.

In the center of it, cupped and huge, was a single raindrop.

She began to cry, looking at it.

They glanced quietly at the sky.

165 "Oh. Oh."

A few cold drops fell on their noses and their cheeks and their mouths. The sun faded behind a stir of mist. A wind blew cool around them. They turned and started to walk back toward the underground house, their hands at their sides, their smiles vanishing away.

170 A boom of thunder startled them and like leaves before a new hurricane, they tumbled upon each other and ran. Lightning struck ten miles away, five miles away, a mile, a half mile. The sky darkened into midnight in a flash.

They stood in the doorway of the underground for a moment until

175 it was raining hard. Then they closed the door and heard the gigantic sound of the rain falling in tons and avalanches, everywhere and forever.

"Will it be seven more years?"

"Yes. Seven."

Then one of them gave a little cry.

180 "Margot!"

"What?"

"She's still in the closet where we locked her."

"Margot."

They stood as if someone had driven them, like so many stakes, into

185 the floor. They looked at each other and then looked away. They glanced out at the world that was raining now and raining and raining steadily. They could not meet each other's glances. Their faces were solemn and pale. They looked at their hands and feet, their faces down.

"Margot."

190 One of the girls said, "Well . . . ?"

No one moved.

"Go on," whispered the girl.

They walked slowly down the hall in the sound of cold rain. They turned through the doorway to the room in the sound of the storm and

195 thunder, lightning on their faces, blue and terrible. They walked over to the closet door slowly and stood by it.

Behind the closet door was only silence.

They unlocked the door, even more slowly, and let Margot out.

C UNDERSTANDING THE STORY

1 Reading Comprehension

Answer these questions to determine how well you understood the story:

1 Why didn't the children like Margot?
2 How does Margot describe the sun in her poem?
3 Why do the children lock Margot in the closet?
4 Why does one of the little girls cry when she feels something on her hand?
5 How do you think the children feel before they open the closet to free Margot?
6 How is the planet Venus described?

2 Guessing Meaning from Context

The words in the list are in the story. Find the words in the story and try to understand their meanings. Match the words with their definitions. Write the letter of the correct definition on the line preceding each vocabulary word.

1	_f_ compounded	a	easing off, lessening
2	___ concussion	b	stifled, covered up
3	___ slackening	c	with great noise
4	___ surged	d	opened and closed both eyes
5	___ muffled	e	pounding
6	___ solemn	f	added to
7	___ blinked	g	strong
8	___ feverish	h	pushed
9	___ savor	i	in a frenzy
10	___ tumbled	j	enjoy, taste
11	___ resilient	k	fell over
12	___ tumultuously	l	serious

3 Grammar: Pronoun Cases: Subjective and Objective

Writers use pronouns to replace nouns. It is important that we always understand what noun the pronoun refers to. Always be aware of this in your writing. First, write the noun you are referring to, and then you can substitute the correct pronoun. Make sure your readers know who he, she, it, or they actually are before you use a pronoun!

In "All Summer in a Day," Bradbury frequently uses the personal pronoun *they* when referring to Margot's classmates: "**They** were all nine years old." Then he switches to *them*: "She heard **them**." Why does the author use *they* in one sentence and *them* in another? *They* is a subject pronoun and *them* is an object pronoun.

This grammatical construction is called pronoun case. Unlike nouns, personal pronouns have different cases. You must use *I*, for example, if the pronoun is the subject of the sentence and *me* if the word is the object. Remember: The subject of a sentence is the person or thing that is the *doer* of the action.

Example:
Margot recalled her days on Earth.

Margot is the subject because she *recalls* her days. If we were to use a pronoun for the noun *Margot*, we would use *she*. Other pronouns in the subjective (or nominative) case are:

SINGULAR	PLURAL
I	we
you	you
who, he, she, it	who, they

Here are some sentences that use subjective case pronouns:

Sam and **he** knew about the third level.
There were only Grace and **she** at the office. (Note: The subject does not always come at the beginning of the sentence.)
My friend and **I** like to travel.
Who is it?

continued

The pronoun *who* can also be a relative pronoun, which means that it relates to a noun or pronoun. In the following sentence, *who* is the subject of the verb *called* and who refers (relates) to woman:

That woman **who** called me yesterday wants to know your name.

The problem with using the subjective or nominative case usually arises when we have double subjects; for example, **Margot and they** were waiting for the sun. If you cross out one of the subjects, such as *Margot and*, you will have no trouble using the correct pronoun, *they*. This sentence means that *Margot* was waiting for the sun, and *they* were waiting for the sun.

Look at this sentence: Both the **narrator and Sam** found the third level. The narrator and Sam are the subjects of this sentence because they are the doers – they found (verb). What did they find? They found *the third level*. *The third level* is the **object** of the sentence because it receives the action from the verb. Pronouns in the objective case are:

Singular	Plural
me	us
you	you
him, her, it	them
whom	whom

Here are some sentences that use objective case pronouns:

The teacher invited **us** for lunch.
She and Grace asked **him** for directions.
Mario and Carlos helped **my mother and me**.
Margot was the girl **whom** they locked in the closet. (Note: *Whom* is the object of the verb *locked*.)

The objective case is also used for objects of prepositions. Prepositions, as you know, are words that indicate direction or relationship. Some commonly used prepositions are: *in, into, on, at, from, for, with, to, between*, and *among*. If you are going to use a pronoun at the end of a prepositional phrase, you must use the objective case:

Mary took her dog with **her**. (object of the preposition *with*)
We bought a gift for Kim and **them**. (object of the preposition *for*)
Let's keep the secret between **you and me**. (object of the preposition *between*)

Application As a review, underline the correct pronoun in each of these sentences.

1 Janet and (<u>she,</u> her) met Tom and (he, <u>him</u>) at the game.
2 My friend and (I, me) thought that Mario and (they, them) were in Spain.
3 That was Momoko (who, whom) you saw on the street yesterday.
4 At the party were Yuko and (they, them).
5 (He, him) and (I, me) found Sara and (she, her) in the library.
6 There is a good relationship between Maggie and (she, her) and between Alan and (he, him).
7 Among the three of (they, them) were Louise and (she, her).
8 We divided the profits between Alan and (he, him).
9 Bill and (we, us) invited Betty and (they, them), (who, whom) you met last summer.
10 The teacher and (he, him) produced the musical play written by the students and (they, them).

4 Editing

To review subjective, objective, and relative pronouns, try this practice exercise. Correct any errors you find in the following paragraph:

My brother Boris and me have a good relationship. It was him whom introduced me to the joys of travel. Every year we go to a new section of the United States. Between him and I we plan a great trip. We traveling together presents no problem. Boris and me get along very well, and he is a person whose tastes are like mines. Boris sends cards to his girlfriend and buys many gifts for ours mother and she. I like to see all the museums and talk to whoever we meet on the trip. When we return, all our friends enjoy us telling our parents and they the stories of our adventures.

D THINKING CRITICALLY

1 Discussing the Story

Discuss the following questions with a partner, in a small group, or with the whole class:

1 Describe Margot. Use as many adjectives as possible.
2 Why doesn't Margot feel comfortable with the other children?
3 What could Margot have done when the children tried to put her in the closet? What would you have done?
4 How different is life on Venus after the sun comes out?
5 How do you think the children in the class feel about Margot after they open the closet?

2 Making Inferences

Authors often write something that is intended to have more than one meaning. While you read, look for meanings that are not explicitly stated – these are inferences. Making inferences will help you enjoy the reading on a different level. The story now has deeper significance, and you will have a better understanding of it.

Read the following lines from the story. Then circle the letter of the best inference.

1 Margot stood apart from them. . . . (line 21)
   a Margot didn't like the other children.
   b Margot was smarter than the other children.
   c Margot was different and felt she didn't belong.

2 "Aw, you didn't write that!" (line 42)
   a The boy is jealous of Margot's poem.
   b Margot doesn't remember how to write.
   c Margot wants to be like the other children.

3 They could not meet each other's glances. (line 187)
   a They now know how Margot feels.
   b Their eyes hurt from seeing the sun.
   c They feel shame for what they did to Margot.

3 Analyzing the Story: Atmosphere

Look back at the Literary Term on page 124. In this story, the writer creates atmosphere through her vivid descriptions of the weather. Look for words in the story that describe the weather on Venus. Write the words and phrases in the circles below.

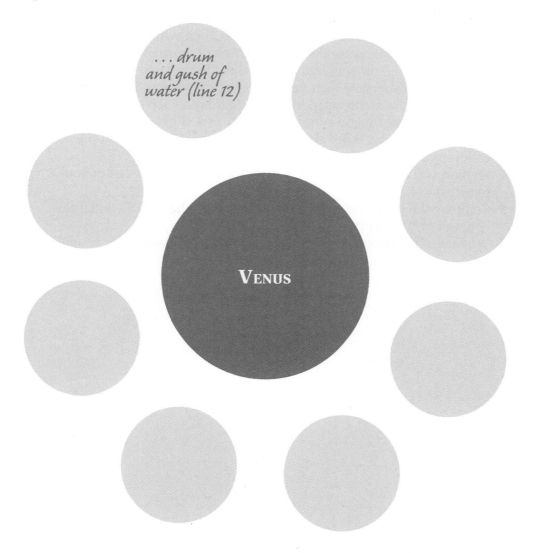

...drum and gush of water (line 12)

VENUS

Pair Discussion   With a partner, compare what you have written. Correct any mistakes you find. How does the atmosphere of the story make you feel?

4 Writing

Read the writing ideas that follow. Your instructor may make specific assignments or ask you to choose one of these:

1 Bradbury creates an intense atmosphere of rain and wetness, which is reinforced throughout the story. Review the story and underline the words that help create this atmosphere. Make a list of opposite words that describe a world of heat and dryness. Then write a story in which sunshine and heat create the setting. Think of yourself as the director of a movie based on your story. What directions would you give the set designers and special effects people? What props would you use?

2 Describe the main character, Margot. What is she like physically and psychologically? Do you sympathize with her? Why?

3 Continue the story. Write about what happens to Margot and the other children.

4 Pretend you are Margot. Write a letter to your classmates after you've returned to Earth.

5 Compare the group behavior in this story with the way the villagers behaved in "The Lottery."

6 Why are some people cruel and discriminatory toward other people?

CHAPTER 9

Désirée's Baby

KATE CHOPIN

A PREPARING TO READ

1 Think Before You Read

Answer the following questions before you read the story:

1 Look up Louisiana in your encyclopedia and find out when it became a state. Who were the first settlers in New Orleans? What is this city famous for?

2 What do you know about the early marriage laws in the southern states? Were they discriminatory?

3 Many nineteenth-century authors used the word *Providence* to mean *God*, as you will note as you read "Désirée's Baby." Other terms you might want to look up are *bayou*, *corbeille*, *layette*, and *peignoir*.

4 How do you think slaves were treated on the average southern plantation? When was slavery declared illegal?

2 Literary Term: Tragedy

A **tragedy** occurs in a story or a play when the main character is defeated by the opposing force at the end of the story. The opposing force can be another person, nature, society, or the character's own personality. For example, in "The Lottery," the opposing force is society, which adheres to a primitive custom of sacrificing a person every year to ensure a good crop. As you read "Désirée's Baby," decide who or what causes the tragedy.

3 Idioms and Expressions

You will find these idioms and expressions in the story:

Providence another name for God	**closing about her** a feeling of being enveloped by something
contained himself tried to be patient	**stole away** left quietly
like a pall a gloomy effect	

B THE STORY

About the Author

Kate Chopin (1851–1904) was born Katherine O'Flaherty in St. Louis, Missouri, to a prosperous Irish-born merchant father and a Creole mother. She learned both French and English, read widely, played the piano, wrote poetry, and lived an independent life. As she grew up, she was greatly admired for her wit and beauty. Among her suitors was Oscar Chopin, a Louisiana cotton trader, whom she married when she was nineteen. They settled first in New Orleans, and then on a plantation near Cloutiersville.

In their twelve years of married life, she bore six children. However, she refused to give up her independence; she dressed unconventionally, smoked cigarettes, and went wherever she pleased unescorted. When her husband died suddenly in 1882, Kate Chopin took over the management of his plantation and turned to writing. She published several short stories, most of them depicting the lives and emotions of southern women in Creole society. Chopin's masterpiece, *The Awakening*, a short novel published in 1899, tells the tragedy of a misunderstood woman in an unfulfilled marriage. You will find much the same theme in "Désirée's Baby."

Désirée's Baby

As the day was pleasant, Madame Valmondé drove over to L'Abri to see Désirée and the baby.

It made her laugh to think of Désirée with a baby. Why, it seemed but yesterday that Désirée was little more than a baby herself; when
5 Monsieur in riding through the gateway of Valmondé had found her lying asleep in the shadow of the big stone pillar.

The little one awoke in his arms and began to cry for "Dada." That was as much as she could do or say. Some people thought she might have strayed there of her own accord, for she was of the toddling age.
10 The prevailing belief was that she had been purposely left by a party of Texans, whose canvas-covered wagon, late in the day, had crossed the ferry that Coton Maïs kept, just below the plantation. In time Madame Valmondé abandoned every speculation but the one that Désirée had been sent to her by a beneficent Providence to be the child of her affection,
15 seeing that she was without child of the flesh. For the girl grew to be beautiful and gentle, affectionate and sincere, – the idol of Valmondé.

It was no wonder, when she stood one day against the stone pillar in whose shadow she had lain asleep, eighteen years before, that Armand Aubigny riding by and seeing her there, had fallen in love with her. That
20 was the way all the Aubignys fell in love, as if struck by a pistol shot. The wonder was that he had not loved her before; for he had known her since his father brought him home from Paris, a boy of eight, after his mother died there. The passion that awoke in him that day, when he saw her at the gate, swept along like an avalanche, or like a prairie fire, or like
25 anything that drives headlong over all obstacles.

Monsieur Valmondé grew practical and wanted things well considered: that is, the girl's obscure origin. Armand looked into her eyes and did not care. He was reminded that she was nameless. What did it matter about a name when he could give her one of the oldest and proudest in
30 Louisiana? He ordered the *corbeille* from Paris, and contained himself with what patience he could until it arrived; then they were married.

Madame Valmondé had not seen Désirée and the baby for four weeks. When she reached L'Abri she shuddered at the first sight of it, as she always did. It was a sad looking place, which for many years had not known the gentle presence of a mistress, old Monsieur Aubigny having married and buried his wife in France, and she having loved her own land too well ever to leave it. The roof came down steep and black like a cowl, reaching out beyond the wide galleries that encircled the yellow stuccoed house. Big, solemn oaks grew close to it, and their thick-leaved, far-reaching branches shadowed it like a pall. Young Aubigny's rule was a strict one, too, and under it his negroes had forgotten how to be gay, as they had been during the old master's easy-going and indulgent lifetime.

> "This is not the baby!" she exclaimed, in startled tones.

The young mother was recovering slowly, and lay full length, in her soft white muslins and laces, upon a couch. The baby was beside her, upon her arm, where he had fallen asleep, at her breast. The yellow nurse woman sat beside a window fanning herself.

Madame Valmondé bent her portly figure over Désirée and kissed her, holding her an instant tenderly in her arms. Then she turned to the child.

"This is not the baby!" she exclaimed, in startled tones. French was the language spoken at Valmondé in those days.

"I knew you would be astonished," laughed Désirée, "at the way he has grown. The little *cochon de lait!*[1] Look at his legs, mamma, and his hands and fingernails, – real fingernails. Zandrine had to cut them this morning. Isn't it true, Zandrine?"

The woman bowed her turbaned head majestically, "Mais si, Madame."[2]

"And the way he cries," went on Désirée, "is deafening. Armand heard him the other day as far away as La Blanche's cabin."

Madame Valmondé had never removed her eyes from the child. She lifted it and walked with it over to the window that was lightest. She scanned the baby narrowly, then looked as searchingly at Zandrine, whose face was turned to gaze across the fields.

"Yes, the child has grown, has changed," said Madame Valmondé, slowly, as she replaced it beside its mother. "What does Armand say?"

Désirée's face became suffused with a glow that was happiness itself.

"Oh, Armand is the proudest father in the parish, I believe, chiefly because it is a boy, to bear his name; though he says not, – that he would have loved a girl as well. But I know it isn't true. I know he

---

[1]**cochon de lait**: piglet, little pig (a term of endearment)
[2]**Mais si, Madame**: Yes, Madam

says that to please me. And mamma," she added, drawing Madame Valmondé's head down to her, and speaking in a whisper, "he hasn't punished one of them – not one of them – since baby is born. Even Négrillon, who pretended to have burnt his leg that he might rest from work – he only laughed, and said Négrillon was a great scamp. Oh, Mamma, I'm so happy; it frightens me."

What Désirée said was true. Marriage, and later the birth of his son had softened Armand Aubigny's imperious and exacting nature greatly. This was what made the gentle Désirée so happy, for she loved him desperately. When he frowned she trembled, but loved him. When he smiled, she asked no greater blessing of God. But Armand's dark, handsome face had not often been disfigured by frowns since the day he fell in love with her.

When the baby was about three months old, Désirée awoke one day to the conviction that there was something in the air menacing her peace. It was at first too subtle to grasp. It had only been a disquieting suggestion; an air of mystery among the blacks; unexpected visits from far-off neighbors who could hardly account for their coming. Then a strange, an awful change in her husband's manner, which she dared not ask him to explain. When he spoke to her, it was with averted eyes, from which the old lovelight seemed to have gone out. He absented himself from home; and when there, avoided her presence and that of her child, without excuse. And the very spirit of Satan seemed suddenly to take hold of him in his dealings with the slaves. Désirée was miserable enough to die.

> When he spoke to her, it was with averted eyes, from which the old love-light seemed to have gone out.

She sat in her room, one hot afternoon, in her *peignoir*, listlessly drawing through her fingers the strands of her long, silky brown hair that hung about her shoulders. The baby, half naked, lay asleep upon her own great mahogany bed, that was like a sumptuous throne, with its satin-lined half-canopy. One of La Blanche's little quadroon boys – half naked too – stood fanning the child slowly with a fan of peacock feathers. Désirée's eyes had been fixed absently and sadly upon the baby, while she was striving to penetrate the threatening mist that she felt closing about her. She looked from her child to the boy who stood beside him, and back again; over and over. "Ah!" It was a cry that she could not help; which she was not conscious of having uttered. The blood turned like ice in her veins, and a clammy moisture gathered upon her face.

She tried to speak to the little quadroon boy; but no sound would come, at first. When he heard his name uttered, he looked up, and his mistress was pointing to the door. He laid aside the great, soft fan, and obediently stole away, over the polished floor, on his bare tiptoes.

120 She stayed motionless, with gaze riveted upon her child, and her face the picture of fright.

Presently her husband entered the room, and without noticing her, went to a table and began to search among some papers which covered it.

125 "Armand," she called to him, in a voice which must have stabbed him, if he was human. But he did not notice. "Armand," she said again. Then she rose and tottered towards him. "Armand," she panted once more, clutching his arm, "look at our child. What does it mean? Tell me."

He coldly but gently loosened her fingers from about his arm and thrust
130 the hand away from him. "Tell me what it means!" she cried despairingly.

"It means," he answered lightly, "that the child is not white; it means that you are not white."

A quick conception of all that this accusation meant for her nerved her with unwonted courage to deny it. "It is a lie; it is not true, I am
135 white! Look at my hair, it is brown; and my eyes are gray, Armand, you know they are gray. And my skin is fair," seizing his wrist. "Look at my hand; whiter than yours, Armand," she laughed hysterically.

"As white as La Blanche's," he returned cruelly; and went away leaving her alone with their child.

140 When she could hold a pen in her hand, she sent a despairing letter to Madame Valmondé.

"My mother, they tell me I am not white. Armand has told me I am not white. For God's sake tell them it is not true. You must know it is not true. I shall die. I must die. I cannot be so unhappy, and live."

145 The answer that came was as brief:

"My own Désirée: Come home to Valmondé; back to your mother who loves you. Come with your child."

When the letter reached Désirée she went with it to her husband's study, and laid it open upon the desk before which he sat. She was like
150 a stone image: silent, white, motionless after she placed it there.

In silence he ran his cold eyes over the written words. He said nothing. "Shall I go, Armand?" she asked in tones sharp with agonized suspense.

"Yes, go."

"Do you want me to go?"

155 "Yes, I want you to go."

He thought Almighty God had dealt cruelly and unjustly with him; and felt, somehow, that he was paying Him back in kind when he stabbed thus into his wife's soul. Moreover he no longer loved her, because of the unconscious injury she had brought upon his home and his name.

She turned away like one stunned by a blow, and walked slowly towards the door, hoping he would call her back.

"Good-bye, Armand," she moaned.

He did not answer her. That was his last blow at fate.

Désirée went in search of her child. Zandrine was pacing the sombre gallery with it. She took the little one from the nurse's arms with no word of explanation, and descending the steps, walked away, under the live-oak branches.

It was an October afternoon; the sun was just sinking. Out in the still fields the negroes were picking cotton.

Désirée had not changed the thin white garment nor the slippers which she wore. Her hair was uncovered and the sun's rays brought a golden gleam from its brown meshes. She did not take the broad, beaten road which led to the far-off plantation of Valmondé. She walked across a deserted field, where the stubble bruised her tender feet, so delicately shod, and tore her thin gown to shreds.

She disappeared among the reeds and willows that grew thick along the banks of the deep, sluggish bayou; and she did not come back again.

●

Some weeks later there was a curious scene enacted at L'Abri. In the centre of the smoothly swept back yard was a great bonfire. Armand Aubigny sat in the wide hallway that commanded a view of the spectacle; and it was he who dealt out to a half dozen negroes the material which kept this fire ablaze.

A graceful cradle of willow, with all its dainty furbishings, was laid upon the pyre, which had already been fed with the richness of a priceless *layette*. Then there were silk gowns, and velvet and satin ones added to these; laces, too, and embroideries; bonnets and gloves; for the *corbeille* had been of rare quality.

The last thing to go was a tiny bundle of letters; innocent little scribblings that Désirée had sent to him during the days of their espousal. There was the remnant of one back in the drawer from which he took them. But it was not Désirée's; it was part of an old letter from his mother to his father. He read it. She was thanking God for the blessing of her husband's love: –

"But, above all," she wrote, "night and day, I thank the good God for having so arranged our lives that our dear Armand will never know that his mother, who adores him, belongs to the race that is cursed with the brand of slavery."

C UNDERSTANDING THE STORY

1 Reading Comprehension

Answer these questions to determine how well you understood the story:

1 Although the story is set in America, why do all of the characters have French names?
2 What makes the reader think, at first, that Armand will be a good husband?
3 At what point in the story do you begin to suspect that there will be a problem?
4 Why does Armand assume that his wife is not a white woman?
5 What is the result of his cruelty to Désirée?
6 Explain the surprise at the end of the story.

2 Guessing Meaning from Context

The words in the list are in the story. Find the words in the story and try to understand their meanings. Write the word that best fits the description. Do not use the same word more than once. Some listed words are not to be used at all.

scanned	beneficent	portly	somber
startled	spectacle	indulgent	unwonted
riveted	sumptuous	suffused	willow
pyre	listless	conception	menacing
corbeille	averted	imperious	

1 a heavyset figure _____*portly*_____

2 a haughty, proud man like Armand _____

3 a threatening gesture _____

4 eyes turned away _____

5 giving a child anything he or she wants _____

6 a kind and generous employer _____

7 a luxurious wedding reception _____

8 a tired feeling _____

9 a sad occasion _____

10 a remarkable sight _____

11 an idea or understanding _____

12 unusual behavior _____

13 a fascinated stare _____

14 spread colors over the sky _____

3 Grammar: Participial Clauses

"Désirée's Baby" contains many participial clauses. A participle is a word that usually ends in *-ing* or *-ed*. It looks like a verb but is used as an adjective, for example, the *running car*. A participial clause is an adjective clause, modifying (describing) a noun or pronoun in the sentence. For example, in the second paragraph of the story, Monsieur Valmondé "found her [Désirée] lying asleep in the shadow of the big stone pillar." What was the pronoun *her* doing? *Lying asleep.* This is a participial clause because it describes a pronoun. The verb *lying* can be both a verb and an adjective. In this case, it is used as an adjective.

Another participial clause occurs in the third paragraph: "seeing she was without child of the flesh." This participial clause describes the word *Providence.*

● Present and past participles Often students are confused by the distinction between participles ending in *-ing* (present) and those ending in *-ed* (past). For example: Are you **interesting** or **interested** in sports? Is your teacher **boring** or **bored**? (We hope neither.) The following discussion may help clear up your confusion.

continued

The present participle gives an active meaning. The noun or pronoun it modifies **does** something.

Example:
That movie was **exciting**.

The movie *caused* excitement (active voice). **The past participle, on the other hand, gives a passive meaning to the noun or pronoun it modifies.**

Example:
The audience was **excited by** the movie.
The *audience* felt excitement (passive voice).

Here are some more examples:

Construction work is **exhausting**. (present participle: The work *causes* exhaustion.)
The construction workers were **exhausted**. (past participle: The *workers* felt exhaustion.)
The South Sea Islands are **fascinating**. (present participle: The islands *cause* fascination.)
We were **fascinated** by the South Sea Islands. (past participle: *We* felt fascination.)

Remember: The present participle causes the result. The past participle reacts to the cause.

Application   Complete the sentences below by using either the present or past participle of the word in parentheses.

(annoy)   **1** We were _____*annoyed*_____ by the constant noise of our neighbor.

2 Our neighbors are always _____*annoying*_____.

(confuse)   **3** That math lesson is _____.

4 I am _____ by the math lesson.

(disgust) **5** John's rude behavior is _____.

6 We were _____ by John's rude behavior.

(frighten) **7** Désirée was _____ by her husband's cold manner.

8 Armand's cold behavior was _____.

(horrify) **9** The earthquakes in Japan and Russia were _____.

10 Readers were _____ by news reports of the earthquakes in Japan and Russia.

(thrill) **11** We were _____ by the enchanting ballet.

12 That ballet performance was _____.

(please) **13** Her soft, melodic voice is _____ to the ear.

14 The audience was _____ by her soft, melodic voice.

(irritate) **15** We were _____ every time we heard his monotonous list of complaints.

16 His monotonous list of complaints is _____.

(amuse) **17** Maria's stories are always _____.

18 Her classmates are always _____ by Maria's stories.

(amaze) **19** Your energy, even at the end of a long day, is _____.

20 I'm _____ by your energy.

D THINKING CRITICALLY

1 Discussing the Story

Discuss the following questions with a partner, in a small group, or with the whole class:

1 How is racism involved in the plot of the story?
2 What personality trait does Armand possess that creates the tragedy? Discuss by giving examples from the story.
3 Discuss the problem of slavery as it existed in the South before the Civil War. How did it eventually divide the Union?
4 Does racism or social class distinction exist in your native country? Explain.

2 Making Inferences

> Authors often write something that is intended to have more than one meaning. While you read, look for meanings that are not explicitly stated – these are inferences. Making inferences will help you enjoy the reading on a different level. The story now has deeper significance, and you will have a better understanding of it.

Read the following lines from the story. Then circle the letter of the best inference.

1 When he spoke to her, it was with averted eyes. . . . (line 97)
   a Armand no longer loves her.
   b Armand doesn't think Désirée is beautiful.
   c Armand has a new lover.

2 She looked from her child to the boy who stood beside him, and back again; over and over. (lines 111–112)
   a Désirée needs glasses.
   b Désirée realizes that her son is the same color as the quadroon boy.
   c Désirée thinks the baby looks like her husband.

3 She disappeared among the reeds and willows . . . and she did not come back again. (lines 177–178)
   a Désirée and the baby died in the swamp.
   b Désirée forgot about Armand and their life together.
   c She put the baby in the swamp.

3 Analyzing the Story: Tragedy

In the late 1800s in the American South, African Americans were enslaved by white land owners. Whites saw themselves as superior to Negroes, as African Americans were called then, and there was intense prejudice against them. Look back at the Literary Term on page 138. This story begins happily and ends in tragedy. Which characters are defeated? What are the opposing forces? What is the story's turning point? Put the following sentences in order and write the numbers on the appropriate lines.

1 Désirée and Armand marry and have a baby.
2 Armand loves Désirée and the baby.
3 Armand Aubigny falls in love with Désirée the first time he sees her.
4 Désirée is found and adopted by Monsieur and Madame Valmondé.
5 The baby's skin is dark.
6 Désirée leaves with the baby.
7 Désirée asks if he wants her to leave.
8 Armand burns the cradle and everything related to the baby and Désirée.
9 Armand reads a letter from his own mother and discovers that the baby's dark skin came from his side of the family, not Désirée's.

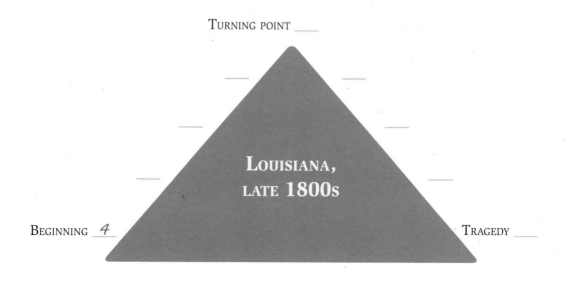

Turning point _____

Beginning _4_

Louisiana, late 1800s

Tragedy _____

Pair Discussion   With a partner, compare what you have written. Correct any mistakes you find. Could there have been a happy ending?

4 Writing

Read the writing ideas that follow. Your instructor may make specific assignments or ask you to choose one of these:

1 Pretend to be Armand and write a defense of your actions.
2 Tell the story from the viewpoint of one of Armand's slaves.
3 Let's suppose that Désirée's baby had survived and he meets his father twenty years later. Write a dialogue between the father and the son.
4 Write a description of a place you have seen that suggests a tragedy could have occurred there.
5 Reread the sixth paragraph of the story, which begins on line 32: "Madame Valmondé had not seen Désirée and the baby for four weeks. When she reached L'Abri she shuddered at the first sight of it, as she always did." Explain, by specific references to the text, how this paragraph foreshadows the tragedy in the story. What other paragraphs or sentences also hint at disaster? Write about this foreshadowing.

A TAKE A CLOSER LOOK

1 Analyzing and Comparing

In each of the following sections, you are asked to think about and compare two of the stories in Part Three.

"All Summer in a Day" and "The Third Level"

- What is the irony in each story? Change the endings so that the irony would be eliminated. Are the stories as effective? Why?
- Contrast the differences in the types of irony used by each author. In which story is the irony tragic? In which story is the irony humorous? Which of the two is more powerful?
- Charley and Margot both want to escape from their environments. Compare the two characters. How are they alike? How are their situations different?

"All Summer in a Day" and "Désirée's Baby"

- Cruelty is a theme in both these stories. Describe the cruelty. Who inflicts the cruelty? Who are the victims?
- Contrast Désirée and Margot as they appear at the beginning of the stories. Which character changes? Why doesn't the other character change?
- How does prejudice bring about tragedy for each character?

"Désirée's Baby" and "The Third Level"

- A letter reveals the ironic endings. Which letter is tragic? Which is humorous?
- How do you think Armand reacted to his mother's letter? What do you think Charley did after receiving the letter from Sam?
- Which ending was more surprising? Which was more realistic?

2 Freewriting

Write the word *anger* in a circle. Think of things that make you angry and write them on lines that radiate from the circle. For fifteen minutes write about people or situations that make you angry and the ways you deal with your anger.

B WORDS FREQUENTLY CONFUSED

From "The Third Level"

In "The Third Level," Charley tries to buy (purchase) a ticket to Galesburg. Do you ever write this word for the preposition *by*? Another *bye* (as in good-bye) can sometimes be confusing, which is also true of the following words from the story. After you have learned their different meanings, write sentences using each word correctly.

> knew (verb), new (adjective)
>
> lead (noun and verb), led (verb)
>
> mail (noun and verb), male (adjective and noun)
>
> sail (noun and verb), sale (noun)

1 _____

2 _____

3 _____

4 _____

5 _____

6 _____

7 _____

8 _____

From "All Summer in a Day"

In this story, the children are nine years old. Frequently, we express the same idea another way: They are *nine-year-old* children. The meaning is the same, but the construction is different. In the first construction, the word *years* is used in the plural form because it is a noun. In the second construction, *nine-year-old* is hyphenated and the *s* is omitted. Because the expression precedes the noun it modifies, the entire expression, *nine-year-old*, is used as an adjective modifying *children*. Note these examples:

three-week vacation   a vacation of three weeks

two-day absence   an absence of two days

five-month-old baby   a baby five months old

Now, look up the following word distinctions from "All Summer in a Day":

sun (noun), son (noun)

remember (verb), memory (noun), remembrance (noun)

always (adverb), all ways (two words: adjective and noun)

pale (adjective), pail (noun)

From "Désirée's Baby"

In this story, Désirée awoke one morning *conscious* that something was wrong. After his terrible act of cruelty, shouldn't Armand's *conscience* have bothered him? Do you know the difference in meaning between these two words? Study the following pairs of similar words and write sentences clearly illustrating their differences:

idol (noun), idle (adjective)

gentle (adjective), genteel (adjective)

mist (noun), missed (verb)

unwonted (adjective), unwanted (adjective)

1 _____

2 _____

3 _____

4 _____

5 _____

6 _____

7 _____

8 _____

C SPELLING

In "The Third Level," Charley *received* a letter from his psychiatrist, Sam. Note the spelling of the word *received*. Do you have trouble getting the *ie* and *ei* words straight? If so, memorize this rhyme: Put *i* before *e* (*niece*) except after *c* (*receive*), or when sounded like *a* as in *neighbor* or *weigh*.

Keeping this pattern in mind, look at the following lists. Practice spelling each of these words by using them in sentences. Or, write a paragraph in which you use at least five *ie* and five *ei* words.

IE		EI	
belief (believe)	friend	ceiling	perceive
brief	grief	conceit	receipt
chief	piece	deceit	reign (an *a* sound)
field	relief (relieve)	freight (an *a* sound)	veign (an *a* sound)

D REVIEW TEST

In each of the following sentences, circle the correct choice:

1 The news of her unexpected marriage was (surprised, surprising).

2 To (who, whom) am I speaking?

3 Margot was the girl (who, whom) remembered the sun.

4 John and Mary had a quarrel. They are no longer speaking to (themselves, each other).

5 My mother and (I, myself) have a good relationship.

6 Between you and (I, me), I don't believe Harry and (he, him).

7 Désirée and (he, him) had a good marriage until the baby was born.

8 That program is so (bored, boring). I want to look at something (interested, interesting).

9 The drilling outside my window is very (annoyed, annoying).

10 I, too, am very (irritated, irritating) by it.

11 Our last speaker told (fascinated, fascinating) tales about his adventures.

12 Your directions are not very clear. We are very (confusing, confused).

13 Let's keep the secret between you and (myself, me).

14 The relationship between Désirée and Armand was very (complicating, complicated).

15 The person (who, whom) you met at my house yesterday was my former teacher.

16 All of the children were cruel to Margot, especially William. It was (he, her) who locked her in the closet.

17 The teacher told Frank and (I, me) a good story.

18 Charley and (myself, I) still believe there is a third level in Grand Central station.

19 Everybody has seen the film except Ted and (me, myself).

20 Jack is very generous to my mother and (I, me).

21 Let's divide the profits among José, Carmen, and (she, her).

22 Phil and (he, him) were chosen to head the committee instead of Ted and (she, her).

23 Before we plan our trip, we need to talk to (each other, ourselves) about what it will cost.

 # WEBQUEST

Find more information about the topics in Part Three by going on the Internet. Go to www.cambridge.org/discoveringfiction/wq and follow the instructions for doing a WebQuest. Have fun. Enjoy the quest!

PART FOUR

Family Relationships

FROM BIRTH until death we have to deal with the first people who come into our lives – our parents and siblings. Even if your home life is essentially happy, there are often still many problems in close relationships. Perhaps you believe that your mother favors your brother or sister, or you don't quite understand your father. Resentments and misunderstandings repressed in childhood can often surface in adult years. Or, conversely, what you once perceived as cruelty can be viewed later as kindness, as you will see in one of the stories from this part.

All three selections in this part deal with the most complex relationships – living day by day with other human beings in a group we call our *family*.

CHAPTER 10

A Visit to Grandmother

WILLIAM MELVIN KELLEY

A PREPARING TO READ

1 Think Before You Read

Answer the following questions before you read the story:

1 It is especially challenging to raise children in a large family. How do parents show their love for each child? How do they avoid playing favorites?
2 In what special ways did your parents show their love for you when you were a child?
3 Did your parents show favoritism to a brother or sister? How did you feel?
4 What are the qualities of a good parent?

2 Literary Term: Conflict

Conflict between characters, ideologies, or countries creates interest in the plot of a story. As readers, we become absorbed in the story and want to see what happens at the end. The conflict can be an internal psychological struggle within one of the characters, or it can be a major eruption between people or nations. Conflict allows the writer to explore and use human emotions such as love, hate, sorrow, joy, and fear.

3 Idioms and Expressions

You will find these idioms and expressions in the story:

go alone join	**laid up** in bed, debilitated
heading to going in a certain direction	**offhand way** casually
	I reckon I guess

B THE STORY

About the Author

William Melvin Kelley (born in 1937) was born in the Bronx, New York, and attended the Fieldston School, a private school in Riverdale. He went on to Harvard University, where he studied under Archibald MacLeish. He describes his desire to write as "a vague undergraduate yearning." After Harvard, however, he was convinced that writing would be his career.

At the age of twenty-five, his first novel, *A Different Drummer*, was published. Reviewers praised the book, and it received the Richard and Hinda Rosenthal Award of the National Institute of Arts and Letters. Additional novels include *A Drop of Patience* (1965), *dem* (1967), and *Dunsford Travels Everywhere* (1970).

Dancers on the Shore, published in 1964, is a collection of short stories, one of which is "A Visit to Grandmother." In the preface to *Dancers on the Shore*, Kelley says, "A writer should ask questions. He should depict people, not symbols or ideas disguised as people."

A Visit to Grandmother

Chig knew something was wrong the instant his father kissed her. He had always known his father to be the warmest of men, a man so kind that when people ventured timidly into his office, it took only a few words from him to make them relax, and even laugh. Doctor Charles Dunford cared about people.

But when he had bent to kiss the old lady's black face, something new and almost ugly had come into his eyes: fear, uncertainty, sadness, and perhaps even hatred.

Ten days before in New York, Chig's father had decided suddenly he wanted to go to Nashville to attend his college class reunion, twenty years out. Both Chig's brother and sister, Peter and Connie, were packing for camp and besides were too young for such an affair. But Chig was seventeen, had nothing to do that summer, and his father asked if he would like to go along. His father had given him additional reasons: "All my running buddies got their diplomas and were snapped up by them crafty young gals, and had kids within a year – now all those kids, some of them gals, are your age."

The reunion had lasted a week. As they packed for home, his father, in a far too offhand way, had suggested they visit Chig's grandmother. "We this close. We might as well drop in on her and my brothers."

So, instead of going north, they had gone farther south, had just entered her house. And Chig had a suspicion now that the reunion had been only an excuse to drive south, that his father had been heading to this house all the time.

His father had never talked much about his family, with the exception of his brother, GL, who seemed part con man, part practical joker, and part Don Juan; he had spoken of GL with the kind of indulgence he would have shown a cute, but ill-behaved and potentially dangerous, five-year-old.

Chig's father had left home when he was fifteen. When asked why, he would answer: "I wanted to go to school. They didn't have a Negro high school at home, so I went up to Knoxville and lived with a cousin and went to school."

They had been met at the door by Aunt Rose, GL's wife, and ushered into the living room. The old lady had looked up from her seat by the window. Aunt Rose stood between the visitors.

The old lady eyed his father. "Rose, who that? Rose?" She squinted. She looked like a doll, made of black straw, the wrinkles in her face running in one direction like the head of a broom. Her hair was white and coarse and grew out straight from her head. Her eyes were brown –

the whites, too, seemed light brown – and were hidden behind thick glasses, which remained somehow on a tiny nose. "That Hiram?" That was another of his father's brothers. "No, it ain't Hiram; too big for Hiram." She turned then to Chig. "Now that man, he look like Eleanor, Charles's wife, but Charles wouldn't never send my grandson to see me. I never even hear from Charles." She stopped again.

"It Charles, Mama. That who it is." Aunt Rose, between them, led them closer. "It Charles come all the way from New York to see you, and brung little Charles with him."

The old lady stared up at them. "Charles? Rose, that really Charles?" She turned away, and reached for a handkerchief in the pocket of her clean, ironed, flowered housecoat, and wiped her eyes. "God have mercy. Charles." She spread her arms up to him, and he bent down and kissed her cheek. That was when Chig saw his face, grimacing. She hugged him; Chig watched the muscles in her arms as they tightened around his father's neck. She half rose out of her chair. "How are you, son?"

Chig could not hear his father's answer.

She let him go, and fell back into her chair, grabbing the arms. Her hands were as dark as the wood, and seemed to become part of it. "Now, who that standing there? Who that man?"

"That's one of your grandsons, Mama." His father's voice cracked. "Charles Dunford, Junior. You saw him once, when he was a baby, in Chicago. He's grown now."

"I can see that, boy!" She looked at Chig squarely. "Come here, son, and kiss me once." He did. "What they call you? Charles too?"

"No, ma'am, they call me Chig."

She smiled. She had all her teeth, but they were too perfect to be her own. "That's good. Can't have two boys answering to Charles in the same house. Won't nobody at all come. So you that little boy. You don't remember me, do you. I used to take you to church in Chicago, and you'd get up and hop in time to the music. You studying to be a preacher?"

"No, ma'am. I don't think so. I might be a lawyer."

"You'll be an honest one, won't you?"

"I'll try."

"Trying ain't enough! You be honest, you hear? Promise me. You be honest like your daddy."

"All right. I promise."

"Good. Rose, where's GL at? Where's that thief? He gone again?"

"I don't know, Mama." Aunt Rose looked embarrassed. "He say he was going by his liquor store. He'll be back."

"Well, then where's Hiram? You call up those boys, and get them over here – now! You got enough to eat? Let me go see." She started to get up. Chig reached out his hand. She shook him off. "What they tell you about me, Chig? They tell you I'm all laid up? Don't believe it.

They don't know nothing about old ladies. When I want help, I'll let you know. Only time I'll need help getting anywheres is when I dies and they lift me into the ground."

She was standing now, her back and shoulders straight. She came only to Chig's chest. She squinted up at him. "You eat much? Your
daddy ate like two men."

"Yes, ma'am."

"That's good. That means you ain't nervous. Your mama, she ain't nervous. I remember that. In Chicago, she'd sit down by a window all afternoon and never say nothing, just knit." She smiled. "Let me see
what we got to eat."

"I'll do that, Mama." Aunt Rose spoke softly. "You haven't seen Charles in a long time. You sit and talk."

The old lady squinted at her. "You can do the cooking if you promise it ain't because you think I can't." Aunt Rose chuckled. "I know you
can do it, Mama."

"All right. I'll just sit and talk a spell." She sat again and arranged her skirt around her short legs.

Chig did most of the talking, told all about himself before she asked. His father only spoke when he was spoken to, and then, only one word
at a time, as if by coming back home, he had become a small boy again, sitting in the parlor while his mother spoke with her guests.

●

When Uncle Hiram and Mae, his wife, came they sat down to eat. Chig did not have to ask about Uncle GL's absence; Aunt Rose volunteered an explanation: "Can't never tell where the man is at. One Thursday
morning he left here and next thing we knew, he was calling from Chicago, saying he went up to see Joe Louis fight. He'll be here though; he ain't as young and footloose as he used to be." Chig's father had mentioned driving down that GL was about five years older than he was, nearly fifty.

Uncle Hiram was somewhat smaller than Chig's father; his short-cropped kinky hair was half gray, half black. One spot, just off his forehead, was totally white. Later, Chig found out it had been that way since he was twenty. Mae (Chig could not bring himself to call her Aunt) was a good deal younger than Hiram, pretty enough so that Chig
would have looked at her twice on the street. She was a honey-colored woman, with long eye lashes. She was wearing a white sheath.

At dinner, Chig and his father sat on one side, opposite Uncle Hiram and Mae; his grandmother and Aunt Rose sat at the ends. The food was good; there was a lot and Chig ate a lot. All through the meal, they talked
about the family as it had been thirty years before, and particularly about the young GL. Mae and Chig asked questions; the old lady answered;

Aunt Rose directed the discussion, steering the old lady onto the best stories; Chig's father laughed from time to time; Uncle Hiram ate.

"Why don't you tell them about the horse, Mama?" Aunt Rose, over Chig's weak protest, was spooning mashed potatoes onto his plate. "There now, Chig."

"I'm trying to think." The old lady was holding her fork halfway to her mouth, looking at them over her glasses. "Oh, you talking about that crazy horse GL brung home that time."

"That's right, Mama." Aunt Rose nodded and slid another slice of white meat on Chig's plate.

Mae started to giggle. "Oh, I've heard this. This is funny, Chig."

●

The old lady put down her fork and began: Well, GL went out of the house one day with an old, no-good chair I wanted him to take over to the church for a bazaar, and he met up with this man who'd just brung in some horses from out West. Now, I reckon you can expect one swindler to be in every town, but you don't rightly think there'll be two, and God forbid they should ever meet – but they did, GL and his chair, this man and his horses. Well, I wished I'd-a been there; there must-a been some mighty highpowered talking going on. That man with his horses, he told GL them horses was half Arab, half Indian, and GL told that man the chair was an antique he'd stole from some rich white folks. So they swapped. Well, I was a-looking out the window and seen GL dragging this animal to the house. It looked pretty gentle and its eyes was most closed and its feet was shuffling.

"GL, where'd you get that thing?" I says.

"I swapped him for that old chair, Mama," he says. "And made myself a bargain. This is even better than Papa's horse."

Well, I'm a-looking at this horse and noticing how he be looking more and more wide awake every minute, sort of warming up like a teakettle until, I swears to you, that horse is blowing steam out its nose.

"Come on, Mama," GL says, "come on and I'll take you for a ride." Now George, my husband, God rest his tired soul, he'd brung home this white folks' buggy which had a busted wheel and fixed it and was to take it back that day and GL says: "Come on, Mama, we'll use this fine buggy and take us a ride."

"GL," I says, "no, we ain't. Them white folks'll burn us alive if we use their buggy. You just take that horse right on back." You see, I was sure that boy'd come by that animal ungainly.

"Mama, I can't take him back," GL says.

"Why not?" I says.

"Because I don't rightly know where that man is at," GL says.

"Oh," I says. "Well, then I reckon we stuck with it." And I turned

around to go back into the house because it was getting late, near
dinnertime, and I was cooking for ten.

"Mama," GL says to my back. "Mama, ain't you coming for a ride
with me?"

"Go on, boy. You ain't getting me inside kicking range of that animal."
I was eyeing that beast and it was boiling hotter all the time. I reckon
maybe that man had drugged it. "That horse is wild, GL," I says.

"No, he ain't. He ain't. That man say he is buggy- and saddle-broke
and as sweet as the inside of an apple."

My oldest girl, Essie, had-a come out on the porch and she says: "Go
on, Mama. I'll cook. You ain't been out the house in weeks."

"Sure, come on, Mama," GL says. "There ain't nothing to be fidgety
about. This horse is gentle as a rose petal." And just then that animal
snorts so hard it sets up a little dust storm around its feet.

"Yes, Mama," Essie says, "you can see he gentle." Well, I looked at
Essie and then at that horse because I didn't think we could be looking
at the same animal. I should-a figured how Essie's eyes ain't never been
so good.

"Come on, Mama," GL says.

"All right," I says. So I stood on the porch and watched GL hitching
that horse up to the white folks' buggy. For a while there, the animal
was pretty quiet, pawing a little, but not much. And I was feeling a little
better about riding with GL behind that crazylooking horse. I could see
how GL was happy I was going with him. He was scurrying around that
animal, buckling buckles and strapping straps, all the time smiling, and
that made me feel good.

Then he was finished, and I must say, that horse looked mighty fine
hitched to that buggy and I knew anybody what climbed up there would
look pretty good too. GL came around and stood at the bottom of the
steps, and took off his hat and bowed and said: "Madam," and reached
out his hand to me and I was feeling real elegant like a fine lady. He
helped me up to the seat and then got up beside me and we moved out
down our alley. And I remember how colored folks come out on their
porches and shook their heads, saying: "Lord now, will you look at Eva
Dunford, the fine lady! Don't she look good sitting up there!" And I
pretended not to hear and sat up straight and proud.

We rode on through the center of town, up Market Street, and all the
way out where Hiram is living now, which in them days was all woods,
there not being even a farm in sight and that's when that horse must-a
first realized he weren't at all broke or tame or maybe thought he was
back out West again, and started to gallop.

"GL," I says, "now you ain't joking with your mama, is you? Because
if you is, I'll strap you purple if I live through this."

Well, GL was pulling on the reins with all his meager strength, and yelling, "Whoa, you. Say now, whoa!" He turned to me just long enough to say, "I ain't fooling with you, Mama. Honest!"

215   I reckon that animal weren't too satisfied with the road, because it made a sharp right turn just then, down into a gulley, and struck out across a hilly meadow. "Mama," GL yells. "Mama, do something!"

    I didn't know what to do, but I figured I had to do something so I stood up, hopped down onto the horse's back and pulled it to a stop.

220 Don't ask me how I did that; I reckon it was that I was a mother and my baby asked me to do something, is all.

    "Well, we walked that animal all the way home; sometimes I had to club it over the nose with my fist to make it come, but we made it, GL and me. You remember how tired we was, Charles?"

225   "I wasn't here at the time." Chig turned to his father and found his face completely blank, without even a trace of a smile or a laugh.

    "Well, of course you was, son. That happened in . . . in . . . it was a hot summer that year and –"

    "I left here in June of that year. You wrote me about it."

230   The old lady stared past Chig at him. They all turned to him; Uncle Hiram looked up from his plate.

    "Then you don't remember how we all laughed?"

    "No, I don't, Mama. And I probably wouldn't have laughed. I don't think it was funny." They were staring into each other's eyes.

235   "Why not, Charles?"

    "Because in the first place, the horse was gained by fraud. And in the second place, both of you might have been seriously injured or even killed." He broke off their stare and spoke to himself more than to any of them: "And if I'd done it, you would've beaten me good for it."

240   "Pardon?" The old lady had not heard him; only Chig had heard.

    Chig's father sat up straight as if preparing to debate. "I said that if I had done it, if I had done just exactly what GL did, you would have beaten me good for it, Mama." He was looking at her again.

    "Why you say that, son?" She was leaning toward him.

245   "Don't you know? Tell the truth. It can't hurt me now." His voice cracked, but only once. "If GL and I did something wrong, you'd beat me first and then be too tired to beat him. At dinner, he'd always get seconds and I wouldn't. You'd do things with him, like ride in that buggy, but if I wanted you to do something with me, you were always

250 too busy." He paused and considered whether to say what he finally did say: "I cried when I left here. Nobody loved me, Mama. I cried all the way up to Knoxville. That was the last time I ever cried in my life."

    "Oh, Charles." She started to get up, to come around the table to him. He stopped her. "It's too late."

255   "But you don't understand."

    "What don't I understand? I understood then; I understand now."

Tears now traveled down the lines in her face, but when she spoke, her voice was clear. "I thought you knew. I had ten children. I had to give all of them what they needed most." She nodded. "I paid more mind
260 to GL. I had to. GL could-a ended up swinging if I hadn't. But you was smarter. You was more growed up than GL when you was five and he was ten, and I tried to show you that by letting you do what you wanted to do."

"That's not true, Mama. You know it. GL was light-skinned and had
265 good hair and looked almost white and you loved him for that."

"Charles, no. No, son. I didn't love any one of you more than any other."

"That can't be true." His father was standing now, his fists clenched tight. "Admit it, Mama . . . please!" Chig looked at him, shocked; the man was actually crying.

270 "It may not-a been right what I done, but I ain't no liar." Chig knew she did not really understand what had happened, what he wanted of her. "I'm not lying to you, Charles."

Chig's father had gone pale. He spoke very softly. "You're about thirty years too late, Mama." He bolted from the table. Silverware and dishes
275 rang and jumped. Chig heard him hurrying up to their room.

They sat in silence for a while and then heard a key in the front door. A man with a new, lacquered straw hat came in. He was wearing brown-and-white two-tone shoes with very pointed toes and a white summer suit. "Say now! Man! I heard my brother was in town. Where he at?
280 Where that rascal?"

He stood in the doorway, smiling broadly, an engaging, open, friendly smile, the innocent smile of a five-year-old.

C UNDERSTANDING THE STORY

1 Reading Comprehension

Answer these questions to determine how well you understood the story:

1 What emotions does Chig see in his father's eyes as Charles kisses his mother?
2 How old is Chig?
3 How old was Charles when he left home?
4 Describe Charles's brother GL.
5 How old was Chig when he had last seen his grandmother?
6 What one word would you use to describe the grandmother?
7 Find a sentence in which the grandmother compliments her son Charles.

2 Guessing Meaning from Context

The words in the list are in the story. Find the words in the story and try to understand their meanings. Write the appropriate word(s) in each sentence. Use each word only once.

crafty	venture	indulgence	swapped
grimaced	fidgety	practical joker	swinging
housecoat	footloose	shuffled	

1 We ____grimaced____ at the sound of her fingernails on the blackboard.

2 The old woman was dressed in a floral _____.

3 She _____ around the kitchen in her slippers and prepared breakfast.

4 The _____ thief moved among the people at the parade.

5 Ben and Jerry _____ stories about their business _____.

6 He treated his inheritance in a casual way and decided to live a(n) _____ , carefree life.

7 The little girl was adored by her father, who offered her every _____ money could buy.

8 Margaret's nervous, _____ behavior made everyone tense.

9 The _____ was an annoyance to his friends because he constantly tried to trick them.

10 The child enjoyed _____ on the old tire.

3 Grammar: Verb Agreement and Collective Nouns

At this stage of learning English, you are probably confident about subject–verb agreement. However, there are some difficult areas that may give you some problems. The following exercises will polish your skills in dealing with collective nouns.

If a subject is singular, the verb must be singular. If the subject is plural, the verb must be plural. Easy? Not always. In some sentences, it is difficult to figure out what the subject of each verb is. Look at this sentence:

The arrival of the tourists seems imminent.

Here, the subject is *arrival*, not tourists. Therefore, the verb must agree with the singular subject, *arrival*. Now look at this sentence:

The tourists seem tired.

Here, the subject is *tourists* (a plural). Therefore, the verb must agree and be plural.

If singular subjects are joined by *either . . . or, neither . . . nor,* the word *or,* or the word *nor,* we use singular verbs.

Examples:
Neither Michelle nor Lisa **has been** to China.
Either the man or the woman **asks** for directions.

If one subject is singular and one is plural, the verb should agree with the subject that is closest.

Example:
Neither my sister nor my brothers **want** to travel this year.

English has many collective nouns that are treated as singular nouns even though they refer to a collection of individuals. Some examples are listed here.

army	chorus	family	jury
audience	class	goverment	orchestra
band	crowd	group	team

Application 1   Underline the subject with one line and the verb with two lines.

1 <u>All</u> the children <u>want</u> toys for Christmas.
2 Each of the pianists is very talented.
3 The color of the roses was so unusual.
4 Mathematics is a challenging subject.
5 Sometimes the news is very depressing.

In sentences 4 and 5, the subjects sound plural but are treated as singular nouns. Look at the box below. These additional words are also considered singular. Use each of them in a sentence. Be sure your subject and verb agree.

aerobics	politics	United States
economics	physics	United Nations

1 _____

2 _____

3 _____

4 _____

5 _____

6 _____

Application 2   Correct the verbs.

1 Neither the coach nor the football players expects _____*expect*_____ to win the game.

2 Either the subway or the buses isn't _____ working today.

3 Neither she nor her friends hopes _____ to win the lottery.

4 I don't know if David or Mark have seen _____ the movie.

5 Neither the bank nor the library are closed _____ today.

6 If my friends or my brother come _____ , I'll call you.

Many English sentences begin with *there is* or *there are*. The word *there* fills in for the actual subject, which occurs later in the sentence.

Application 3   In each sentence that follows, underline the actual subject of the sentence and make sure it agrees with the verb you insert (*is* or *are*).

1 There _____*are*_____ many <u>banks</u> in my city.

2 There _____ a group of children standing near the playground.

3 There _____ some examples of metaphors in the story.

4 There _____ milk in the refrigerator.

5 There _____ neither a letter nor a card in the mailbox.

6 There _____ either a concert or a dance recital every week at school.

7 There _____ questions nobody can answer.

8 There _____ good news about his job interview.

Other words or phrases that take singular verbs include *each, every, everyone, everybody, anyone, anybody, one of,* and *each of.*

Examples:
Everybody **is** responsible for her own actions.
Each of the spectators **hopes** the team will win.

Application 4   Write the correct verb(s).

1 One of my sisters _____*works*_____ (work, works) at a television station.

2 Every member of the orchestra _____ (practice, practices) three hours a day.

3 Each of the children _____ (want, wants) a toy for Christmas.

4 One of my favorite foods _____ (is, are) chocolate.

5 Anyone who _____ (know, knows) her _____
(like, likes) her.

6 Everyone she asked _____ (feel, feels) enthusiastic about
the trip.

Application 5   Look back at the list of collective nouns on page 168. Use
each one in a sentence.

1 _____

2 _____

3 _____

4 _____

5 _____

6 _____

7 _____

8 _____

9 _____

10 _____

11 _____

12 _____

D THINKING CRITICALLY

1 Discussing the Story

Discuss the following questions with a partner, in a small group, or with the whole class:

1 Why does Charles want to visit his family after his long absence?
2 Why does Charles bring Chig with him?
3 How does Charles feel about his mother?
4 What did he want from her as a child?
5 What is the significance of the story about the runaway horse? What purpose does this story serve in the plot?
6 What do we know about GL? Describe him.
7 Does Chig like his grandmother? Explain your answer.

2 Making Inferences

> Authors often write something that is intended to have more than one meaning. While you read, look for meanings that are not explicitly stated – these are inferences. Making inferences will help you enjoy the reading on a different level. The story now has deeper significance, and you will have a better understanding of it.

Read the following lines from the story. Then circle the letter of the best inference.

1 Chig knew something was wrong the instant his father kissed her. (line 1)
   a His father does not like his grandmother.
   b His father is shy about kissing his own mother in public.
   c His father isn't very affectionate to anyone.

2 "They don't know nothing about old ladies." (line 85)
   a People don't realize how tough old ladies can be.
   b People like old ladies.
   c Old ladies want to be independent.

3 His father only spoke when he was spoken to . . . as if by coming back home, he had become a small boy again. . . . (line 104–105)
   a His father was experiencing the hurt he felt as a young boy.
   b Chig thinks of his father as being a young boy again.
   c Chig's father wanted to be young again.

3 Analyzing the Story: Conflict

Look back at the Literary Term on page 159. Think about the conflict between the mother and son. How do the two characters feel about the events in the past? Find each line below in the story, and write the words and phrases that show how the other character feels about the event described.

CHARLES	MAMA
1	You remember how tired we was, Charles? (line 224)
2	Then you don't remember how we all laughed? (line 232)
3 I said that if I had done it . . . you would have beaten me good for it, Mama. (lines 241–243)	
4	I paid more mind to GL. I had to. (lines 259–260)
5 GL was light-skinned and had good hair . . . and you loved him for that. (lines 264–265)	

Pair Discussion   With a partner, compare what you have written. Correct any mistakes you find. What emotion do you think the author is exploring in the story?

4 Writing

Read the writing ideas that follow. Your instructor may make specific assignments or ask you to choose one of these:

1 What do you think Chig is feeling as he observes the confrontation between his father and grandmother at the dinner table? Write about Chig's feelings.
2 Create a conversation between Chig and Charles later that evening or the next day.
3 Write an essay in which Chig describes his grandmother to one of his friends when he gets back home.
4 GL is not a fully developed character in this story, and yet he serves an important role. Discuss his significance to the plot.
5 Compare and contrast the relationship between Charles and Chig and Charles and his mother.
6 Describe the conflict in this story and discuss whether or not you think it is resolved by the end of the story.

CHAPTER 11

Too Soon a Woman

Dorothy M. Johnson

A **PREPARING TO READ**

1 Think Before You Read

Answer the following questions:

1 What do you know about pioneer life in America's West?
2 What qualities of character would have been helpful to pioneers beginning a new life in the West?
3 Look up the meaning of the following terms that apply to the early settlers: *prairie*, *homesteader*, *teamster*, and *covered wagon*.
4 What dangers do you think pioneers faced?
5 Why would it be unwise to eat a mushroom you found in the woods?

2 Literary Term: Characterization

Every story depends on **characters** to develop the plot. The actions, personalities, and subconscious motivations of these characters make us, the readers, interested in them. The author reveals characters through physical descriptions, dialogues, thoughts, feelings, and the observations of other characters. As you read "Too Soon a Woman," see what you learn about the main character from the observations of the narrator.

3 Idioms and Expressions

You will find these idioms and expressions in the story:

two-bit of small worth	**hide nor hair** a trace of something
grub food	**all-fired (all fired up)** enthusiastic
rigged up put together	**plumb** completely

B THE STORY

About the Author

Dorothy M. Johnson (1905–1984) lived all of her life in the West. She was born in McGregor, Iowa, and later moved to Montana, where she attended the state university. After graduating from college, she worked as an editor at several magazines until 1952, when she was appointed as professor of journalism at Montana State University. During and after her time as editor, she wrote many short stories, which she incorporated into a book entitled *The Hanging Tree*. The principal story in this collection was made into a movie in 1959. At that time, Johnson had also written a novel, *Buffalo Woman*, for which she received an award from the Western Writers of America. In 1969 she wrote a biography of Sitting Bull, the famous Indian. The book so pleased the Blackfoot tribe that they made her an honorary member.

Johnson's work has been praised for its realism and strong characters, like the protagonist (the main character) in "Too Soon a Woman."

Too Soon a Woman

We left the home place behind, mile by slow mile, heading for the mountains, across the prairie where the wind blew forever.

At first there were four of us with the one-horse wagon and its skimpy load. Pa and I walked, because I was a big boy of eleven. My two little
5 sisters romped and trotted until they got tired and had to be boosted up into the wagon bed.

That was no covered Conestoga, like Pa's folks came West in, but just an old farm wagon, drawn by one weary horse, creaking and rumbling westward to the mountains, toward the little woods town where Pa
10 thought he had an old uncle who owned a little two-bit sawmill.

Two weeks we had been moving when we picked up Mary, who had run away from somewhere that she wouldn't tell. Pa didn't want her along, but she stood up to him with no fear in her voice.

"I'd rather go with a family and look after kids," she said, "but I ain't
15 going back. If you won't take me, I'll travel with any wagon that will."

Pa scowled at her, and her wide blue eyes stared back.

"How old are you?" he demanded.

"Eighteen," she said. "There's teamsters come this way sometimes. I'd rather go with you folks. But I won't go back."

20 "We're prid'near[1] out of grub," my father told her. "We're clean out of money. I got all I can handle without taking anybody else." He turned away as if he hated the sight of her. "You'll have to walk," he said.

So she went along with us and looked after the little girls, but Pa wouldn't talk to her.

25 On the prairie, the wind blew. But in the mountains, there was rain. When we stopped at little timber claims along the way, the homesteaders said it had rained all summer. Crops among the blackened stumps were rotted and spoiled. There was no cheer anywhere, and little hospitality. The people we talked to were past worrying. They were scared and desperate.

30 So was Pa. He traveled twice as far each day as the wagon, ranging through the woods with his rifle, but he never saw game. He had been depending on venison. But we never got any except as a grudging gift from the homesteaders.

He brought in a porcupine once, and that was fat meat and good.
35 Mary roasted it in chunks over the fire, half crying with the smoke. Pa and I rigged up the tarp sheet for shelter to keep the rain from putting the fire clean out.

The porcupine was long gone, except for some of the tried-out fat that Mary had saved, when we came to an old, empty cabin. Pa said we'd

---

[1]**prid'near**: pretty near (almost)

⁴⁰ have to stop. The horse was wore out, couldn't pull anymore up those grades on the deep-rutted roads in the mountains.

At the cabin, at least there was shelter. We had a few potatoes left and some corn meal. There was a creek that probably had fish in it, if a person could catch them. Pa tried it for half a day before he gave up. To this day I don't care for fishing. I remember my father's sunken eyes in his gaunt, grim face.

He took Mary and me outside the cabin to talk. Rain dripped on us from branches overhead.

"I think I know where we are," he said. "I calculate to get to old John's and back in about four days. There'll be grub in the town, and they'll let me have some whether old John's still there or not."

He looked at me. "You do like she tells you," he warned. It was the first time he had admitted Mary was on earth since we picked her up two weeks before.

"You're my pardner," he said to me, "but it might be she's got more brains. You mind what she says."

He burst out with bitterness. "There ain't anything good left in the world, or people to care if you live or die. But I'll get grub in the town and come back with it."

He took a deep breath and added, "If you get too all-fired hungry, butcher the horse. It'll be better than starvin'."

He kissed the little girls good-bye and plodded off through the woods with one blanket and the rifle.

The cabin was moldy and had no floor. We kept a fire going under a hole in the roof, so it was full of blinding smoke, but we had to keep the fire so as to dry out the wood.

The third night we lost the horse. A bear scared him. We heard the racket, and Mary and I ran out, but we couldn't see anything in the pitch-dark.

In gray daylight I went looking for him, and I must have walked fifteen miles. It seemed like I had to have that horse at the cabin when Pa came or he'd whip me. I got plumb lost two or three times and thought maybe I was going to die there alone and nobody would ever know it, but I found the way back to the clearing.

That was the fourth day, and Pa didn't come. That was the day we ate up the last of the grub.

The fifth day, Mary went looking for the horse. My sisters whimpered, huddled in a quilt by the fire, because they were scared and hungry.

I never did get dried out, always having to bring in more damp wood and going out to yell to see if Mary would hear me and not get lost. But I couldn't cry like the little girls did, because I was a big boy, eleven years old.

It was near dark when there was an answer to my yelling, and Mary came into the clearing.

85   Mary didn't have the horse – we never saw hide nor hair of that old horse again – but she was carrying something big and white that looked like a pumpkin with no color to it.

    She didn't say anything, just looked around and saw Pa wasn't there yet, at the end of the fifth day.

90   "What's that thing?" my sister Elizabeth demanded.

    "Mushroom," Mary answered. "I bet it hefts ten pounds."

    "What are you going to do with it now?" I sneered. "Play football here?"

    "Eat it – maybe," she said, putting it in a corner. Her wet hair hung over her shoulders. She huddled by the fire.

95   My sister Sarah began to whimper again. "I'm hungry!" she kept saying.

    "Mushrooms ain't good eating," I said. "They can kill you."

    "Maybe," Mary answered. "Maybe they can. I don't set up to know all about everything, like some people."

    "What's that mark on your shoulder?" I asked her. "You tore your
100 dress on the brush."

    "What do you think it is?" she said, her head bowed in the smoke.

    "Looks like scars," I guessed.

    "'Tis scars. They whipped me. Now mind your own business. I want to think."

105   Elizabeth whimpered, "Why don't Pa come back?"

    "He's coming," Mary promised. "Can't come in the dark. Your pa'll take care of you soon's he can."

    She got up and rummaged around in the grub box.

    "Nothing there but empty dishes," I growled. "If there was anything,
110 we'd know it."

    Mary stood up. She was holding the can with the porcupine grease. "I'm going to have something to eat," she said coolly. "You kids can't have any yet. And I don't want any squalling, mind."

    It was a cruel thing, what she did then. She sliced that big, solid
115 mushroom and heated grease in a pan.

    The smell of it brought the little girls out of their quilt, but she told them to go back in so fierce a voice that they obeyed. They cried to break your heart.

    I didn't cry. I watched, hating her.

120   I endured the smell of the mushroom frying as long as I could. Then I said, "Give me some."

    "Tomorrow," Mary answered. "Tomorrow, maybe. But not tonight." She turned to me with a sharp command: "Don't bother me! Just leave me be."

125   She knelt there by the fire and finished frying the slice of mushroom.

    If I'd had Pa's rifle, I'd have been willing to kill her right then and there.

    She didn't eat right away. She looked at the brown, fried slice for a while and said, "By tomorrow morning, I guess you can tell whether you want any."

130　　The little girls stared at her as she ate. Sarah was chewing an old leather glove.

　　When Mary crawled into the quilts with them, they moved away as far as they could get.

　　I was so scared that my stomach heaved, empty as it was.

135　　Mary didn't stay in the quilts long. She took a drink out of the water bucket and sat down by the fire and looked through the smoke at me.

　　She said in a low voice, "I don't know how it will be if it's poison. Just do the best you can with the girls. Because your pa will come back, you know. . . . You better go to bed. I'm going to sit up."

140　　And so would you sit up. If it might be your last night on earth and the pain of death might seize you at any moment, you would sit up by the smoky fire, wide-awake, remembering whatever you had to remember, savoring life.

　　We sat in silence after the girls had gone to sleep. Once I asked, "How
145　long does it take?"

　　"I never heard," she answered. "Don't think about it."

　　I slept after a while, with my chin on my chest. Maybe Peter dozed that way at Gethsemane as the Lord knelt praying.

　　Mary's moving around brought me wide-awake. The black of night
150　was fading.

　　"I guess it's all right," Mary said. "I'd be able to tell by now, wouldn't I?"

　　I answered gruffly, "I don't know."

　　Mary stood in the doorway for a while, looking out at the dripping world as if she found it beautiful. Then she fried slices of the mushroom
155　while the little girls danced with anxiety.

　　We feasted, we three, my sisters and I, until Mary ruled, "That'll hold you," and would not cook any more. She didn't touch any of the mushroom herself.

　　That was a strange day in the moldy cabin. Mary laughed and was
160　gay; she told stories, and we played "Who's Got the Thimble?" with a pine cone.

　　In the afternoon we heard a shout, and my sisters screamed and I ran ahead of them across the clearing.

　　The rain had stopped. My father came plunging out of the woods
165　leading a pack horse – and well I remember the treasures of food in that pack.

　　He glanced at us anxiously as he tore at the ropes that bound the pack.

　　"Where's the other one?" he demanded.

　　Mary came out of the cabin then, walking sedately. As she came
170　toward us, the sun began to shine.

　　My stepmother was a wonderful woman.

1 Reading Comprehension

Answer these questions to determine how well you understood the story:

1 Why didn't the father in the story want to let Mary come along with his family?
2 Where was the family going? How do we know that they were poor?
3 Why wouldn't she let the children eat the mushroom at first? When did she finally cook it for them?
4 Give three examples of Mary's courage.
5 Explain the meaning of the last sentence in the story.
6 How does the title of this story explain Mary's situation?

2 Guessing Meaning from Context

The words below are in the story. Find the words in the story and try to understand their meanings. Look at the four definitions for each word and circle the correct one.

1 romp
   a play actively   **c** jump
   b sit quietly   **d** shout

2 boosted
   a bragged   **c** raised up
   b lowered   **d** tied together

3 scowl
   a look with displeasure   **c** smile
   b scold   **d** protect

4 gaunt
   a fall   **c** thin
   b gruesome   **d** unhappy

5 grim
   a frightened   **c** harsh
   b dirty   **d** suffering

6 plod
   a run quickly   **c** explore
   b walk heavily   **d** plan

7 moldy
  a small animal
  b damp
  c shapely
  d stale

8 whimper
  a cry softly
  b plead
  c scream
  d face bravely

9 grudgingly
  a generously
  b giving reluctantly
  c selfishly
  d in a hospitable manner

10 savor
  a keep for future use
  b substitute
  c cook with skill
  d taste with pleasure

11 sedately
  a producing sleepiness
  b noisily
  c in a dignified manner
  d rushing forward

12 skimpy
  a large
  b move with leaps
  c deficient in size
  d cheap

3 Grammar: Conditional Sentences and Expressing Requests and Wishes

The subjunctive mood is more commonly found in conditional sentences. Conditional sentences are categorized as future conditional, present conditional, or past conditional.

● Future conditional We use the future conditional when we refer to something that may happen in the future if a certain condition exists. *If* introduces the conditional clause and the verb is in the simple present or present progressive tense. The result clause (what will happen if the condition exists) is in the future tense, and the future tense verb is often accompanied by a modal.

Examples:
  If I **buy** a ticket, I **may win** the lottery.
  If she **leaves** now, she **will be** on time for her job.
  If he **is running** for Congress, he **will need** volunteers.

continued

If the conditional clause comes at the beginning of the sentence, it must be separated from the result clause with a comma. However, the order of the clauses may be reversed. Then, no comma is used to separate the clauses.

Examples:
I may win the lottery if I buy a ticket.
She will be on time for her job if she leaves now.

In the future conditional, it is possible that things can happen. We use the present tense of the verb even though we are indicating a future action.

INCORRECT: If I will study, I will succeed in school.
CORRECT: **If I study, I will succeed** in school.

● Present conditional We use the present conditional when we refer to how situations might be different from the way they are now. Sometimes, this conditional is called the contrary to fact, or unreal, conditional.

Examples:
If I **were** a bird, I **could fly**. (I am not a bird. I can't fly.)
If they **had** money, they **would travel**. (They don't have money. They won't travel.)

The conditional clause uses the past tense, and the result clause uses *would* + the base form of the verb.

When the verb *be* occurs in a present conditional clause, we use *were* for both singular and plural subjects.

Example:
If **I were** a bird, I would fly.
If **we were** birds, we would fly.

● Past conditional Present and future conditionals are possible situations: If you do something in the present, something may happen in the future. Past conditionals, however, are impossible situations. We use the past conditional when we are guessing about how things might have been different in the past. We are altering the past by going back in time. The *if*-clause uses the verb in the past perfect tense (*had* + the past participle). The main clause uses *would have, could have,* or *should have* + the past participle.

Examples:
"If I'd had Pa's rifle, I'd have been willing to kill her right then and
   there." (from the story)
If he had gone with his friends, he could have seen the
   football game.

● Expressing requests and wishes We use conditional forms to show
conditions under which something may happen in the present, past,
or future. We also use the conditional form for polite requests and
wishes.

Examples:
I would like to sit down.
Would you like to go to the movies?
Should we try this new restaurant?

Application 1   Finish the following sentences by writing a result clause.

1 If I finish my homework,

  I *will go out* _____.

2 If she tells the police about the money she found,

  they _____.

3 If we take a shortcut to the airport,

  _____.

4 If you lend me your car,

  _____.

5 If you are polite to people,

  _____.

Rewrite the preceding sentences by putting the result clause before the conditional (*if*) clause. Do not put a comma between the clauses!

1 _____

2 _____

3 _____

4 _____

5 _____

Application 2   Combine each pair of sentences into one present conditional sentence.

1 She doesn't know how to dance. She can't enter the contest.

If she knew how to dance, she could enter the contest.

2 We don't speak Chinese. We can't converse with our Chinese neighbor.

_____

3 They don't know where the treasure is buried. They don't have a map.

_____

4 I am not the president. I can't declare a war on drugs.

_____

5 It's not raining. I'm not carrying an umbrella.

_____

6 I am not you. I won't call your mother.

_____

Application 3 Combine each pair of sentences into one past conditional sentence.

1 We weren't home. We didn't watch the program.

If we had been home, we would have watched the program.

2 I wasn't at the lecture. I didn't hear the professor speak about geopolitics.

3 He didn't pay attention to the rules. He didn't stay in the company.

4 Our team didn't practice every day. We didn't win the championship game.

5 Bill and Eva didn't enjoy the concert. They didn't stay until the end.

6 Brad didn't go to Paris. He didn't see the Eiffel Tower.

Application 4 Write sentences using polite conditionals.

1 *Would you like to order dinner now?*

2

3

4

5

Application 5 You may work with a partner or in a group. List some popular superstitions using future conditional sentences.

1 *If you break a mirror, you will have bad luck for seven years.*

2 _____

3 _____

4 _____

5 _____

6 _____

7 _____

8 _____

9 _____

Application 6 Using the present conditional, list some of the things you would, could, or should do.

If I won the lottery,

I would _____

I could _____

I should _____

If I were invisible,

I would _____

I could _____

I should _____

Application 7   Using the past conditional, list some of the things you would have, should have, or could have done.

If I had known my future,

I would have _____

I could have _____

I should have _____

D THINKING CRITICALLY

1 Discussing the Story

Discuss the following questions with a partner, in a small group, or with the whole class:

1 Why do you think Mary ran away? Why wouldn't she tell what happened to her?
2 Why does the author tell the story from the viewpoint of an eleven-year-old boy?
3 How do we know that the narrator is recalling the story many years after it happened?
4 How does the title describe Mary?
5 Give examples from the story that show a change in the boy's attitude toward Mary.
6 Explain the effect produced by these sentences: "Mary came out of the cabin then, walking sedately. As she came toward us, the sun began to shine."

2 Making Inferences

Authors often write something that is intended to have more than one meaning. While you read, look for meanings that are not explicitly stated – these are inferences. Making inferences will help you enjoy the reading on a different level. The story now has deeper significance, and you will have a better understanding of it.

Read the following lines from the story. What can you infer about character, setting, plot, or theme? Write your answer on the line below.

1 . . . Mary, who had run away from somewhere that she wouldn't tell. (lines 11–12)

Mary ran away from a terrible situation and doesn't want to be sent back there.

2 . . . she stood up to him with no fear in her voice. (line 13)

She wasn't shy

3 . . . Pa wouldn't talk to her. (lines 23–24)

He didn't believe him

4 She looked at the brown, fried slice for a while and said, "By tomorrow morning I guess you can tell whether you want any." (lines 127–129)

5 Mary stood in the doorway . . . looking out at the dripping world as if she found it beautiful. (lines 153–154)

3 Analyzing the Story: Characterization

Look back at the Literary Term on page 175. The author characterizes Mary through physical descriptions, dialogue, thoughts, feelings, and observations from other characters. In the boxes below, find words and phrases from the story to describe Mary.

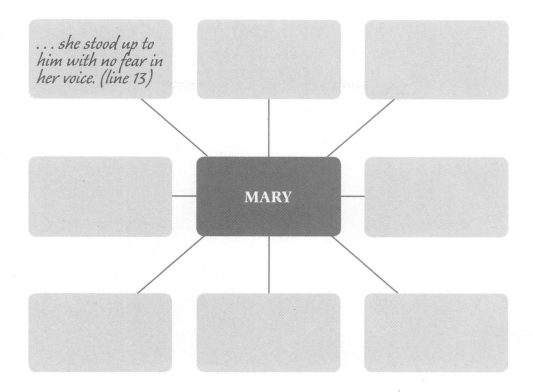

...she stood up to him with no fear in her voice. (line 13)

MARY

Pair Discussion   With a partner, compare what you have written. Correct any mistakes you find. How would you describe Mary? Draw the diagram above on a separate piece of paper and add your own words.

4 Writing

Read the writing ideas that follow. Your instructor may make specific assignments or ask you to choose one of these:

1 The story is told by an unnamed narrator, an eleven-year-old boy. Write it from Mary's viewpoint or from Pa's.
2 Write Mary's thoughts as she sat up all night waiting to find out if the mushroom was poisonous.
3 Make up a dialogue creating a scene that is suggested but does not actually occur in the story, for example, Pa falling in love with Mary, their wedding day, or Mary's relationship with her stepson.
4 Comment on this statement: "One must sometimes be cruel in order to be kind." Write about how this refers to "Too Soon a Woman," to any other story you may have read, or to an incident in your own life.
5 Read another story about pioneer life and compare it in character and theme to "Too Soon a Woman." Some suggestions are the stories of Willa Cather or Bret Harte, or other stories by Dorothy Johnson in her collection, *The Hanging Tree.*

CHAPTER 12

Thicker Than Water

RALPH HENRY BARBOUR

A PREPARING TO READ

1 Think Before You Read

Answer the following questions before you read the story:

1 Have you ever been in a hospital? Were you a patient or a visitor?
2 What is a blood transfusion? In what circumstances do doctors usually give a blood transfusion?
3 Have you ever donated blood? What were the circumstances? How did you feel afterwards?
4 Would you ever sacrifice your own life to save someone else? If yes, who would you do this for?

2 Literary Term: Suspense

Suspense is a technique in which an author creates a situation that keeps the reader guessing the outcome of the events that make up the plot. Suspense is achieved by the author's method of delaying the climax through dialogue, description, or the main character's physical or mental reactions. As you read the story, notice how the sentences which describe the boy's mental stress create suspense.

3 Idioms and Expressions

You will find these idioms and expressions in the story:

make (my) excuses explain the situation and apologize for my absence	**put it strong** be extremely persuasive
pull through live (not die)	**quit beefin'** stop worrying; complaining
mighty little time not much time	**Your sacrifice has won!** The blood transfusion was successful!
(his) face lighted he looked optimistic or hopeful	**How soon do I croak?** When do I die?

B THE STORY

About the Author

Ralph Henry Barbour (1870–1944), wrote over 100 novels and numerous short stories for boys that stressed the importance of teamwork and school spirit. Some of his best stories appeared in the magazines *Boys' Life* and *The American Boy*.

Barbour was born and bred in Massachusetts very close to Harvard University. However, he never attended Harvard but chose to go to a military academy in Worchester where he wrote poetry. He discovered, he said, "that certain words sounded alike and could be set down on paper in such a manner that certain editors called them verse and paid good money for them."

Before graduation, he sold many poems and jingles to weekly magazines under the pseudonym Richard Stillman Powell.

From his early success with poetry, he went on to become a reporter for newspapers in Boston, Denver, Chicago, and Philadelphia. Always loving sports, Barbour wrote his first novel, *The Half-Back*, a football story in which the substitute wins the game. The novel sold so well that Barbour gave up newspaper work to write sports stories full time. He never lost interest in athletics and in boys who were heroes. His most famous short story was one he heard from an acquaintance, George Osborne, and which Barbour entitled "Thicker Than Water," published in 1899. The story by Barbour and Osborne won first prize in *Life* magazine's short story contest in 1916.

There is little known of George Osborne. Even Ralph Barbour lost track of him.

Thicker Than Water

Doctor Burroughs, summoned from the operating room, greeted his friend from the doorway: "Sorry, Harry, but you'll have to go on without me. I've got a case on the table that I can't leave. Make my excuses, will you?"

5   "There's still an hour," replied the visitor. "I'm early and can wait."

"Then come in with me." Markham followed to the operating room, white-walled, immaculate, odorous of stale ether and antiseptics. On the table lay the sheeted form of a young girl. Only the upper portion of the body was visible, and about the neck wet, red-stained bandages

10   were bound. "A queer case," said the surgeon. "Brought here from a sweat-shop two hours ago. A stove-pipe fell and gashed an artery in her neck. She's bleeding to death. Blood's supposed to be thicker than water, but hers isn't, poor girl. If it would clot she might pull through. Or I could save her by transfusion, but we can't find any relatives, and

15   there's mighty little time."

The attending nurse entered. "The patient's brother is here," she announced, "and is asking to see her."

"Her brother!" The surgeon's face lighted. "What's he like?"

"About twenty, Doctor; looks strong and healthy."

20   "See him, Nurse. Tell him the facts. Say his sister will die unless he'll

give some blood to her. Or wait!" He turned to Markham. "Harry, you do it! Persuasion's your line. Make believe he's a jury. But put it strong, old man! And hurry! Every minute counts!"

The boy was standing stolidly in the waiting-room, only the pallor of his healthy skin and the anxiety of his clear eyes hinting at the strain. Markham explained swiftly, concisely.

"Doctor Burroughs says it's her one chance," he ended.

The boy drew in his breath and paled visibly.

"You mean Nell'll die if someone don't swap his blood for hers?"

"Unless the blood she has lost is replaced—"

"Well, quit beefin'," interrupted the other roughly. "I'm here, ain't I?"

When he entered the operating room the boy gave a low cry of pain, bent over the form on the table, and pressed his lips to the white forehead. When he looked up his eyes were filled with tears. He nodded to the surgeon.

Doggedly, almost defiantly, he submitted himself, but when the artery had been severed and the blood was pulsing from his veins to the inanimate form beside him his expression changed to that of abject resignation. Several times he sighed audibly, but as if from mental rather than bodily anguish. The silence became oppressive. To Markham it seemed hours before the surgeon looked up from his vigil and nodded to the nurse. Then:

"You're a brave lad," he said cheerfully to the boy. "Your sacrifice has won!"

The boy, pale and weak, tried to smile. "Thank God!" he muttered. Then, with twitching mouth: "Say, Doc, how soon do I croak?"

"Why, not for a good many years, I hope." The surgeon turned frowningly to Markham. "Didn't you explain that there was no danger to him?"

"God! I'm afraid I didn't!" stammered Markham. "I was so keen to get his consent. Do you mean that he thought—"

The surgeon nodded pityingly and turned to the lad. "You're not going to die," he said gently. "You'll be all right tomorrow. But I'm deeply sorry you've suffered as you must have suffered the past hour. You were braver than any of us suspected!"

"Aw, that's all right," muttered the boy. "She's my sister, ain't she?"

C UNDERSTANDING THE STORY

1 Reading Comprehension

Answer these questions to determine how well you understood the story:

1 What happened to the young girl at the sweat-shop? What will happen to her if she doesn't get a blood transfusion?
2 Who is Markham? What job does he do?
3 How does the boy react when he sees his sister?
4 Is the blood transfusion painful? Why or why not?
5 What did the boy think was going to happen to him? Why did he think this?
6 Who explains the truth to the boy? How does the boy react to this news?

2 Guessing Meaning from Context

The words in the list are in the story. Find the words in the story and try to understand their meanings. Match the words from the first column with the definitions in the second column by writing the letter of the best meaning to the left of each word. There are more meanings than there are words. After you finish the matching exercise, select one word from the list, and write a paragraph using that word to describe a person or a situation.

1	_f_ immaculate	**a**	rhythmic flow of something
2	___ make believe	**b**	an expression of unhappiness
3	___ pallor	**c**	acceptance of a bad situation
4	___ concisely	**d**	unemotionally
5	___ pulse	**e**	with determination
6	___ inanimate	**f**	very clean
7	___ resignation	**g**	acute sorrow
8	___ doggedly	**h**	pretend
9	___ anguish	**i**	not moving, lifeless
10	___ severed	**j**	with enthusiasm
		k	briefly and clearly stated
		l	a pale color to the skin
		m	cut

3 Grammar: Possessive Pronouns and Contractions

At the beginning of "Thicker Than Water," the nurse tells the doctor "The patient's brother is here." The apostrophe is used to indicate the possessive case ("the *patient's* brother.")

We usually show possession in nouns by using either an apostrophe (') followed by an *s* or a possessive pronoun.

Example:
"**Her** brother!" The surgeon's face lighted.

The possessive pronouns (*my, your, his, her, its, our, your,* and *their*) are used as modifiers and precede a noun. It is important not to confuse these possessive pronouns with possessive pronouns that function as nouns (*mine, yours, his, hers, its, ours, yours,* and *theirs*).

Example:
"You mean Nell'll die if someone won't swap **his** blood for **hers**."
INCORRECT: Hers blood won't clot.
CORRECT: **Her** blood won't clot.
The problem was **hers**.

SINGULAR		PLURAL	
I	my, mine	we	our, ours
you	your, yours	you	your, yours
he	his	they	their, theirs
she	her, hers		
it	its		

A common problem with possessive pronouns is the proper use of *its*. Do not confuse *its* and *it's*. Possessive pronouns do not require an apostrophe. The word *it's* with the apostrophe is a contraction for *it is*. *Its* without the apostrophe is a possessive pronoun referring to things, places or animals.

Example:
The patient was injured by a broken stove-pipe. **Its** fall severed her artery.

In "Thicker Than Water," Doctor Burroughs tells his friend, "Sorry, Harry, but you'll have to go without me. I've got a case on the table that I can't leave."

continued

We use an apostrophe to form the contraction (*you'll, I've*) rather than use full helping verbs (*you will, I have*) and to show missing letters (*can't* instead of *cannot*).

Why does the author use contractions? This is because in dialogue, contractions are the most natural way of speaking.

Application 1   Read the sentences, and underline the correct pronoun in parentheses. Compare your answers with a partner.

1 The river draws (<u>its</u>, it's) water from many sources.
2 The books you found in the gym are (our, ours).
3 (Its, It's) too bad Tom didn't study for the test. He could have passed it.
4 Have you seen our new magazine? The drawing on the cover is (mine, your).
5 My sister has a blue bike. I have a red one. The yellow one is (your, yours).
6 (My, Mine) house needs repair. (Its, It's) roof is leaking.
7 This is my pen. The blue one is (hers, her) pen.
8 Is the house with the red door (his, her)?
9 No, that house is (theirs, their).

Application 2   Write ten sentences using possessive pronouns in the singular and the plural. Write some sentences with possessive pronouns before a noun and write some sentences using possessive pronouns that function as nouns. Compare your work with a partner.

4 Editing

Correct the following paragraph for errors in the use of possessive pronouns and the use of apostrophes. There are (6) errors to find.

Surgeons must have special skill's. It is essential that doctors keep up to date with new knowledge about procedures for operating on patients. Its not unusual for unexpected emergencies to occur. Doctors must decide whether it's necessary to perform an operation or use medication. They should respond quickly and efficiently. A career in medicine also means a doctor should be willing to sacrifice his or hers social life. A hospital's reputation depends on it's staff. If you want to be a physician, you must consider some hardships', such as inconvenient, long hours. However, many doctors find great satisfaction in knowing that theirs work saves lives.

D THINKING CRITICALLY

1 Discussing the Story

Discuss the following questions with a partner, in a small group, or with the whole class:

1 There is a saying, "Blood is thicker than water." What does this mean? How does this apply to what you have just read?
2 The reader knows that the patient's name is Nell, but we don't know the boy's name. Why do you think the author chooses not to reveal his name?
3 How does the boy's comment at the end of the story explain the meaning of the title?
4 Why does the boy's misunderstanding of what he was asked to do make him a hero?
5 At what point in the story does the boy think he is going to die? How do you know?

2 Making Inferences

> Authors often write something that is intended to have more than one meaning. While you read, look for meanings that are not explicitly stated – these are inferences. Making inferences will help you enjoy the reading on a different level. The story now has deeper significance, and you will have a better understanding of it.

Read the following lines from the story. What can you infer about character, setting, plot, or theme? Write your answer on the line below.

1 "Blood's supposed to be thicker than water, but hers isn't, poor girl." (lines 12–13)

The girl is in danger of dying because her blood won't clot.

2 "Doctor Burroughs says it's her one chance." (line 27)

_____

3 When he entered the operating room the boy gave a low cry of pain. . . . (lines 32–33)

---

4 . . . his expression changed to that of abject resignation. (lines 38–39)

---

5 Several times he sighed audibly, but as if from mental rather than bodily anguish. (lines 39–40)

---

3 Analyzing the Story: Suspense

Whether the girl will live or die and the brother's obvious mental anguish throughout the story keep the reader guessing the outcome. This creates suspense. Look back at the Literary Term on page 191. The following chart shows the building of suspense in the story. The plot points are listed below the chart. Show where the plot points go in the chart by writing the numbers in the appropriate places. An example has been done for you.

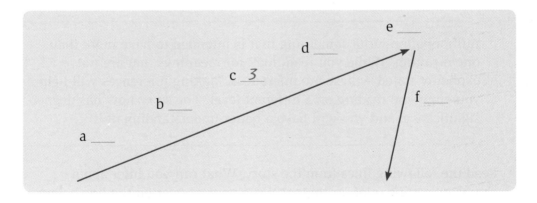

1 The boy learns that his sister is very close to death and he becomes very anxious.
2 Markham realizes his mistake and Doctor Burroughs explains to the boy that he's not going to die.
3 Doctor Burroughs asks Markham to persuade the brother to give blood.
4 The girl is bleeding heavily and there is little time to save her life.
5 Markham and the boy wait anxiously for the boy to give blood.
6 Markham enters the operating room and sees Nell.

Pair Discussion   With a partner, compare what you have written in your charts. Correct any mistakes. Discuss how the story would have been different if the doctor had spoken to the boy instead of Markham when the boy first arrived at the hospital.

4 Writing

Read the writing ideas that follow. Your instructor may make specific assignments or ask you to choose one of these:

1 Pretend to be the girl's brother. Write your thoughts as you agree to donate your blood to your sister.
2 Construct the scene in which Markham uses strong persuasion to convince the boy to agree to the transfusion.
3 Write a dialogue between Nell and her brother when she becomes conscious after the transfusion.
4 What do you think Doctor Burroughs told his wife when he came late to his social engagement? Write the scene that occurred between them.
5 Suppose Ralph Henry Barbour suddenly meets George Osborne after ten years. Write their dialogue when Barbour tells his friend about the success of their story.

A TAKE A CLOSER LOOK

1 Analyzing and Comparing

In the next sections, you are asked to think about and compare two of the stories in Part Four. In the final section, compare all three stories.

"A Visit to Grandmother" and "Too Soon a Woman"

- How are the families in each of the stories similar? How are they different?
- Compare the grandmother from "A Visit to Grandmother" with Mary from "Too Soon a Woman."
- How do these women relate to children? How do they show their love and concern?

"Thicker Than Water" and "A Visit to Grandmother"

Compare the relationship between the brother and sister in the Barbour story with the relationship between Charles and his mother.

- How close is the relationship between the brother and sister? What is the brother afraid of? How well do Doctor Burroughs and Markham communicate with the brother?
- How well do the mother and son understand each other? How do they communicate? Does their reunion help or hurt their relationship?

All Three Stories

- What is the conflict in each story?
- Are the lines of communication improved at the end of each story? How?
- How does the theme of misunderstanding form the plot of each story?

2 Freewriting

Communication and its effect on family relationships is a theme in each of the stories in Part Four. Write the word *family* on a piece of paper. Now write any words you associate with the word *family*. Write for fifteen minutes about your own family.

B WORDS FREQUENTLY CONFUSED

From "A Visit to Grandmother"

In this story, Charles cannot *excuse* his mother's *excuses* of GL's outrageous behavior. Notice the use of the same word as both a verb and a noun. The following pairs of words also occur in "A Visit to Grandmother." Write sentences correctly using each of them. Since you have learned the rules of subject and verb agreement in this chapter, test your knowledge by underlining the subject of each sentence with one line and the verb with two lines.

    weak (adjective), week (noun)

    bazaar (noun), bizarre (adjective)

    beat (verb), beet (noun)

1 _____

2 _____

3 _____

4 _____

5 _____

6 _____

From "Too Soon a Woman"

The boy in the story is *scared* that Mary will die from eating the mushroom. Mary's arm is *scarred* from the whipping she received. What is the difference in meaning between the two words? There is also another word, *sacred*, that you would use when referring to religion, church, or holy things. Here are some other groups of words that might confuse you. Write sentences correctly using each of them.

    four (adjective), fourth (adjective), forth (adverb)

    break (noun and verb), brake (noun and verb)

    pain (noun and verb), pane (noun)

1 _____

2 _____

3 _____

4 _____

5 _____

6 _____

7 _____

From "Thicker Than Water"

The nurse in the story announces: "The patient's brother is here." What is the difference between *patient* and *patience*? Write sentences using the following pairs of words from "Thicker Than Water."

it's (pronoun and verb), its (possessive pronoun)

vein (noun), vain (adjective)

your (possessive pronoun), you're (pronoun)

1 _____

2 _____

3 _____

4 _____

5 _____

6 _____

C SPELLING

Forming the Present Participle

From the spelling patterns for Part One, you learned not to drop the final vowel of a verb to form the past tense. For example, *care* became *cared* in the past; *hope* became *hoped*. However, when adding the suffix *-ing*, we must do the opposite: We must drop the final vowel before adding *-ing*. *Care* becomes *caring*, and *hope* becomes *hoping*. Here are some other examples:

PRESENT	PAST	PRESENT PARTICIPLE
date	dated	dating
injure	injured	injuring
dine	dined	dining

For the past tense of most verbs ending in *y*, we change the *y* to *i* (unless the *y* is preceded by a vowel) and add *-ed*. *Study*, for instance, becomes *studied*. When adding *-ing* to the root word (when forming the present participle), we keep the *y*. *Study* becomes *studying*. More examples follow:

PRESENT	PAST	PRESENT PARTICIPLE
reply	replied	replying
worry	worried	worrying
try	tried	trying

As a review, complete the following chart by writing each verb in its past tense and present participle form:

PRESENT	PAST	PRESENT PARTICIPLE
say		
envy		
cry		
suppose		
judge		
dry		
raise		
arrive		
produce		
graduate		

REVIEW TEST

Some of the following sentences are correct; others contain an error (or errors) in the use of possessives, subject-verb agreement, or conditionals. If the sentence is correct, write the letter *C* in the space below each sentence. If the sentence is incorrect, underline the error or errors and rewrite the sentence correctly. For example,

INCORRECT: Not one of us <u>want</u> to go to the game.

CORRECT: Not one of us **wants** to go to the game.

1 Charles, Chig's father, rarely visit his own mother.

_____

2 Here come Jack and Jill.

_____

3 If we had the money, we would buy a more expensive car.

_____

4 Its too bad that it rained yesterday. We had to cancel the game.

_____

5 Dickens novels are famous in every country.

_____

6 Neither you nor I are to blame.

_____

7 Every one of us are responsible.

_____

8 Each of us does good work.

_____

9 The treasure is jewels.

_____

10 Chig, as well as his father, were surprised to see GL.

_____

11 Charles's mother thinks she understand her son.

_____

12 If it don't rain, we'll go to the park.

_____

13 Your going to the game, aren't you?

_____

14 If the mushroom were poisonous, Mary would have died.

_____

15 My name is Susan. What's your?

_____

16 The son and his father understands each other.

_____

17 If Pa hadn't allowed Mary to join the family, the children will
have starved.

_____

WEBQUEST

Find more information about the topics in Part Four by going on the Internet.
Go to www.cambridge.org/discoveringfiction/wq and follow the instructions
for doing a WebQuest. Have fun. Enjoy the quest!

PART FIVE

Meeting Challenges

IN THE LATTER part of the twentieth century, human beings challenged the universe. We landed on the moon, penetrated the mysteries of space, developed computer technology to a science, climbed mountains, and made remarkable archaeological discoveries. All challenges, however, do not have to be physical or phenomenal. Every day we take up small challenges; we fight daily battles of our own.

There are innumerable situations that have tested you since the days of your childhood: your first day at school, meeting new friends, and adjusting to unfamiliar environments. Currently, you might be competing for a job or trying to break a bad habit. Whatever you are facing now, you should be able to relate to the challenges of the characters in this final part of the book.

CHAPTER 13
A Rice Sandwich
SANDRA CISNEROS

CHAPTER 14
The Circus
WILLIAM SAROYAN

CHAPTER 15
The Warriors
ANNA LEE WALTERS

A Rice Sandwich

SANDRA CISNEROS

A PREPARING TO READ

1 Think Before You Read

Answer the following questions before you read the story:

1 Think back to when you were a young child. Was there something you wanted very much? How did you convince your parents to give it to you?
2 Did you ever cry in school because you were embarrassed or afraid? How did you cope with your emotions?
3 How did other people react to your tears?
4 What are your memories of your early school days? Did you like or dislike school?

2 Literary Term: Tone

Tone shows the mood of the story. It reflects the author's attitude, which may be serious, humorous, romantic, or even tragic. In "A Rice Sandwich," Cisneros treats the main character with affection and humor and thereby establishes the tone of the story.

3 Idioms and Expressions

You will find these idioms and expressions in the story:

get to eat be allowed to eat	**I bet** I have a strong feeling
got it in my head had an idea	**next thing you know** soon, the result will be
get to go have an opportunity to go	

B THE STORY

About the Author

The daughter of a Mexican father and a Mexican American mother, Sandra Cisneros was born in Chicago in 1954. After graduating from college, she worked as a teacher to high school dropouts, and she also wrote poetry and short stories. Her poems and fiction won her two fellowships in creative writing, and she later taught creative writing at several Midwest colleges.

Cisneros is the author of four books of poetry and two books of short stories, *The House on Mango Street* and *Woman Hollering Creek.* She often dedicates her books to her mother, whom she calls "la smart cookie." As you read the story, think about whether the mother of the main character might be based on the author's parent.

A Rice Sandwich

The special kids, the ones who wear keys around their necks, get to eat in the canteen. The canteen! Even the name sounds important. And these kids at lunch time go there because their mothers aren't home or home is too far away to get to.

5   My home isn't far but it's not close either, and somehow I got it in my head one day to ask my mother to make me a sandwich and write a note to the principal so I could eat in the canteen too.

Oh no, she says pointing the butter knife at me as if I'm starting trouble, no sir. Next thing you know everybody will be wanting a bag
10   lunch – I'll be up all night cutting bread into little triangles, this one with mayonnaise, this one with mustard, no pickles on mine, but mustard on one side please. You kids just like to invent more work for me.

But Nenny says she doesn't want to eat at school – ever – because she likes to go home with her best friend Gloria who lives across the
15   schoolyard. Gloria's mama has a big color T.V. and all they do is watch cartoons. Kiki and Carlos, on the other hand, are patrol boys. They don't want to eat at school either. They like to stand out in the cold especially if it's raining. They think suffering is good for you ever since they saw that movie "300 Spartans."

20   I'm no Spartan and hold up an anemic wrist to prove it. I can't even blow up a balloon without getting dizzy. And besides, I know how to make my own lunch. If I ate at school, there'd be less dishes to wash. You would see me less and less and like me better. Everyday at noon my chair would be empty. Where is my favorite daughter you would cry, and
25   when I came home finally at 3 p.m. you would appreciate me.

Okay, okay, my mother says after three days of this. And the following morning I get to go to school with my mother's letter and a rice sandwich because we don't have lunch meat.

Mondays or Fridays, it doesn't matter, mornings always go by slow
30   and this day especially. But lunch time came finally and I got to get in line with the stay-at-school kids. Everything is fine until the nun who knows all the canteen kids by heart looks at me and says: you, who sent you here? And since I am shy, I don't say anything, just hold out my hand with the letter. This is no good, she says, till Sister Superior gives
35   the okay. Go upstairs and see her. And so I went.

I had to wait for two kids in front of me to get hollered at, one because he did something in class, the other because he didn't. My turn came and I stood in front of the big desk with holy pictures under the glass while the Sister Superior read my letter. It went like this:

40   Dear Sister Superior, Please let Esperanza eat in the lunch room because she lives too far away and she gets tired. As you can see she is

very skinny. I hope to God she does not faint. Thanking you, Mrs. E. Cordero.

45   You don't live far, she says. You live across the boulevard. That's only four blocks. Not even. Three maybe. Three long blocks away from here. I bet I can see your house from my window. Which one? Come here. Which one is your house?

And then she made me stand up on a box of books and point. That
50   one? she said pointing to a row of ugly 3-flats, the ones even the raggedy men are ashamed to go into. Yes, I nodded even though I knew that wasn't my house and started to cry. I always cry when nuns yell at me, even if they're not yelling.

Then she was sorry and said I could stay – just for today, not
55   tomorrow or the day after – you go home. And I said yes and could I please have a Kleenex – I had to blow my nose.

In the canteen, which was nothing special, lots of boys and girls watched while I cried and ate my sandwich, the bread already greasy and the rice cold.

C UNDERSTANDING THE STORY

1 Reading Comprehension

Answer these questions to determine how well you understood the story:

1 Who is the narrator of the story?
2 Why does Esperanza want to eat in the canteen?
3 Why doesn't the mother want to make a sandwich for Esperanza?
4 Who are Kiki and Carlos?
5 What happens when Esperanza tries to blow up a balloon?
6 How does Esperanza convince her mother to write a note to the principal?
7 Why doesn't the nun allow her to have lunch in the canteen every day? Do you think Esperanza is disappointed by this decision? Explain.

2 Guessing Meaning from Context

The words in the list on page 212 are in the story. Find the words in the story and try to understand their meanings. For each definition, write the correct word on the line. Notice that you have been given the part of speech with each definition.

Spartan	canteen	anemic	nodded
skinny	dizzy	hollered	
raggedy	faint	boulevard	
nun	greasy	suffer	

1 *boulevard* wide street (noun)

2 _____ swoon, pass out (verb)

3 _____ to endure, be in pain (verb)

4 _____ very thin (adjective)

5 _____ yelled (verb)

6 _____ worn out, tattered (adjective)

7 _____ weak, lacking enough red blood cells (adjective)

8 _____ cafeteria (noun)

9 _____ self-disciplined, not afraid of pain or danger

10 _____ moved the head downward to signal approval (verb)

11 _____ unsteady (adjective)

12 _____ a woman who is a member of a religious order (noun)

13 _____ oily (adjective)

3 Grammar: Simple, Compound, and Complex Sentences

In Part Four, you learned about subject-verb agreement, and you focused on simple sentences. A simple sentence must have at least one subject and one verb and must express a complete thought. As we become more proficient in a language, we speak and write in more complex sentences.

A compound sentence has at least two main clauses. Each clause has its own subject and verb and can stand on its own (an independent clause). This is a compound sentence:

My home isn't far, but it's not close either.

In this sentence, the two independent (main) clauses are joined by the conjunction *but*. Other conjunctions are *and, or, nor, so (therefore), for (because)*, and *yet (but)*. When a conjunction joins two independent clauses, it should be preceded by a comma.

A complex sentence consists of one independent clause with one or more dependent clauses.

Example:
When the siren wailed, I jumped.

In this sentence, "When the siren wailed" is the dependent clause, and "I jumped" is the independent clause.

Certain words act as markers or flags that signal the beginning of a dependent clause. Some of these words are: *who, whom, whose, which*, and *that*. These pronouns are called relative pronouns. They introduce clauses that modify (describe) nouns.

Application 1 Use a conjunction to combine the simple sentences into compound sentences. Underline the subject of each clause once and the verb twice.

1 We like to go to the movies. We like to see Broadway shows.

We like to go to the movies, and we like to see Broadway shows.

2 He waited a long time for the train. He was late for work.

3 She looked in the mailbox for his letter. He had not written to her.

4 Please let Esperanza eat in the lunch room. She lives too far away.

---

5 I was a good runner. I ran as hard as I could.

---

6 We hope it doesn't snow. We won't be able to get home.

---

7 We liked the movie. The book was better.

---

8 They planned a surprise party for Anna. They sent out invitations.

Who and *whom* refer to people: *who* is the subjective case, *whom* is the objective case. *Whose* is a possessive pronoun that is used for people, animals, and things. *Which* and *that* are interchangeable. In informal speech, *that* is sometimes used for *who*.

Examples:
The girl **who** borrowed the library book never returned it.
Mr. Gold, **whom** I have always admired, is a dynamic speaker.
The neighbors complained about the dog **whose** barking kept
   them awake.

Other words and phrases also serve as markers or flags and introduce dependent clauses. These include: *after, as, as long as, although, because, before, even if, even though, if, since, unless, until, when, whenever, whether,* and *while.* If a clause marker comes before the main or independent clause, it must be followed by a comma (as in the sentence you just read). Clause markers do not need a comma when they follow the main clause (as shown in this sentence).

Application 2   Underline the subject in each clause with one line and the verb with two lines. Then circle the clause marker that introduces the dependent clause.

1 (When) the <u>astronauts</u> <u>landed</u>, the <u>people</u> <u>cheered</u> and <u>clapped</u>.

2 Because I am shy, I don't say anything.

3 Nenny doesn't want to eat at school because she likes to go home with Gloria.

4 I stood in front of the big desk while the Sister Superior read my letter.

5 You would appreciate me when I came home finally at 3 p.m.

6 Lots of boys and girls watched while I ate my sandwich.

Now change the order of the clauses in the preceding sentences. Remember to punctuate properly.

1 _____

2 _____

3 _____

4 _____

5 _____

6 _____

D THINKING CRITICALLY

1 Discussing the Story

Discuss the following questions with a partner, in a small group, or with the whole class:

1 Describe Esperanza. Use as many adjectives as you can.
2 In what ways are you like Esperanza when you try to get things you want?
3 How does the mother show she is sensitive to Esperanza's desires?
4 Discuss the reaction of the nuns to Mrs. Cordero's letter.
5 Why does Esperanza cry?

2 Making Inferences

Authors often write something that is intended to have more than one meaning. While you read, look for meanings that are not explicitly stated – these are inferences. Making inferences will help you enjoy the reading on a different level. The story now has deeper significance, and you will have a better understanding of it.

Read the following lines from the story. Then circle the letter of the best inference.

1 The canteen! Even the name sounds important. (line 2)
   a Esperanza likes to speak English.
   b Esperanza doesn't like her mother's cooking.
   c Esperanza thinks eating in the canteen will be a special experience.

2 I always cry when nuns yell at me, even if they're not yelling. (line 52–53)
   a Esperanza is very shy.
   b Esperanza cries easily.
   c Esperanza is afraid of the nuns.

3 In the canteen . . . lots of boys and girls watched while I cried and ate my sandwich. . . . (line 57–58)
   a Esperanza's adventure was a disappointment.
   b Esperanza wants to be back home.
   c Esperanza knows her mother is always right.

3 Analyzing the Story: Tone

Look back at the Literary Term on page 209. Think about the tone of the story. Read the story again and decide if the following sentences in the story convey a humorous or serious tone. Put them in the correct columns.

The special kids . . . get to eat in the canteen. (lines 1–2)
You kids just like to invent more work for me. (line 12)
I can't even blow up a balloon without getting dizzy. (lines 20–21)
If I ate at school, there'd be less dishes to wash. (line 22)
Where is my favorite daughter you would cry. . . . (line 24)
As you can see she is very skinny. (lines 41–42)
I hope to God she does not faint. (line 42)
. . . then she made me stand up on a box of books and point. (line 49)
I always cry when nuns yell at me, even if they're not yelling.
(lines 52–53)

HUMOROUS	SERIOUS
	The special kids . . . get to eat in the canteen.

Pair Discussion   With a partner, compare what you have written. Correct any mistakes you find. Can you add any more examples of humorous or serious tone?

4 Writing

Read the writing ideas that follow. Your instructor may make specific assignments or ask you to choose one of these:

1 Write an essay describing the relationship between Esperanza and her mother.
2 What do you think the nuns should have said to Esperanza? Write a dialogue that is different from the one in the story.
3 Are teachers as sensitive to children as they should be? Write about a teacher you remember who was very thoughtful and kind to you.
4 What are the qualities of a good teacher? Imagine that you are a teacher, and write about how you would treat your students.
5 What does Esperanza learn? Write a sentence that describes the moral of the story and then elaborate on your idea.
6 Compare Esperanza to Margot from "All Summer in a Day."

CHAPTER 14

The Circus

WILLIAM SAROYAN

A PREPARING TO READ

1 Think Before You Read

Answer the following questions before you read the story:

1 What do you think of when you hear the word *circus*?
2 Why do you think people join a circus?
3 When spring comes, do you notice a difference in the way people behave? What is the difference?
4 If you could be anywhere else right now, where would you want to be?
5 As you read this story, try to remember what you were like when you were in fifth grade (ten or eleven years old).

2 Literary Term: Dialogue

An author will often use **dialogue** (conversation) to develop the plot of a story. This story has a lot of dialogue, much of which is written in a regional dialect. The characters become even more real when we hear them speak to each other.

3 Idioms and Expressions

You will find these idioms and expressions in the story:

run hog-wild be wild	**figured** thought
give us a hand help	**came tearing into** ran quickly into a place
going to the dogs becoming bad	
whacks hits, slaps	**by rights** correctly, as one should
pulling for all we were worth using all our energy	**on account of** because
powerful strapping strong whipping	**cussing** cursing

B THE STORY

About the Author

William Saroyan (1908–1981) was descended from an Armenian family that settled in Fresno, California. As a teenager, he decided to be a writer. He sold his first story to a Boston newspaper, and it was later included in the anthology *Best Short Stories of 1934*. "The Daring Young Man on the Flying Trapeze" was the story that made Saroyan famous. In 1940, Saroyan won the Pulitzer Prize for his play, *The Time of Your Life*.

Saroyan's characters are based on his relatives and members of the community from his childhood. The strong influence of the family is felt in the stories, and there are often conflicts between ethnic family values and the desire to assimilate into American culture.

My Name Is Aram, the novel from which the story "The Circus" is taken, is one of Saroyan's most popular works. It is a coming-of-age book set in the 1940s in California, but it is universal in its insights about a young boy's development.

The Circus

Any time a circus used to come to town, that was all me and my old pal Joey Renna needed to make us run hog-wild, as the saying is. All we needed to do was see the signs on the fences and in the empty store windows to start going to the dogs and neglecting our educations.
5 All we needed to know was that a circus was on its way to town for me and Joey to start wanting to know what good a little education ever did anybody anyway.

After the circus reached town we were just no good at all. We spent all our time down at the trains, watching them unload the animals, walking
10 out Ventura Avenue with the wagons with lions and tigers in them and hanging around the grounds, trying to win the favor of the animal men, the workers, the acrobats, and the clowns.

The circus was everything everything else we knew wasn't. It was adventure, travel, danger, skill, grace, romance, comedy, peanuts,
15 popcorn, chewing-gum and soda-water. We used to carry water to the elephants and stand around afterwards and try to seem associated with the whole magnificent affair, the putting up of the big tent, the getting everything in order, and the worldly-wise waiting for the people to come and spend their money.

20 One day Joey came tearing into the classroom of the fifth grade at Emerson School ten minutes late, and without so much as removing his hat or trying to explain his being late, shouted, Hey, Aram, what the hell are you doing here? The circus is in town.

And sure enough I'd forgotten. I jumped up and ran out of the room
25 with poor old Miss Flibety screaming after me, Aram Garoghlanian, you stay in this room. Do you hear me, Aram Garoghlanian?

I heard her all right and I knew what my not staying would mean. It would mean another powerful strapping from old man Dawson. But I couldn't help it. I was just crazy about a circus.

30 I been looking all over for you, Joey said in the street. What happened?

I forgot, I said. I knew it was coming all right, but I forgot it was today. How far along are they?

I was at the trains at five, Joey said. I been out at the grounds since seven. I had breakfast at the circus table. Boy, it was good.

Honest, Joey? I said. How were they?

They're all swell, Joey said. Couple more years, they told me, and I'll be ready to go away with them.

As what? I said. Lion-tamer, or something like that?

I guess maybe not as a lion-tamer, Joey said. I figure more like a workman till I learn about being a clown or something, I guess. I don't figure I could work with lions right away.

We were out on Ventura Avenue, headed for the circus grounds, out near the County Fairgrounds, just north of the County Hospital.

Boy, what a breakfast, Joey said. Hot-cakes, ham and eggs, sausages, coffee. Boy.

Why didn't you tell me? I said.

I thought you knew, Joey said. I thought you'd be down at the trains same as last year. I would have told you if I knew you'd forgotten. What made you forget?

I don't know, I said. Nothing, I guess.

I was wrong there, but I didn't know it at the time. I hadn't really forgotten. What I'd done was remembered. I'd gone to work and remembered the strapping Dawson gave me last year for staying out of school the day the circus was in town. That was the thing that had kind of kept me sleeping after four-thirty in the morning when by rights I should have been up and dressing and on my way to the trains. It was the memory of that strapping old man Dawson had given me, but I didn't know it at the time. We used to take them strappings kind of for granted, me and Joey, on account of we wanted to be fair and square with the Board of Education and if it was against the rules to stay out of school when you weren't sick, and if you were supposed to get strapped for doing it, well, there we were, we'd done it, so let the Board of Education balance things the best way they knew how. They did that with a strapping. They used to threaten to send me and Joey to Reform School but they never did it.

Circus? old man Dawson used to say. I see. Circus. Well, bend down, boy.

So, first Joey, then me, would bend down and old man Dawson would get some powerful shoulder exercise while we tried not to howl. We wouldn't howl for five or six licks, but after that we'd howl like Indians coming. They used to be able to hear us all over the school and old man Dawson, after our visits got to be kind of regular, urged us politely to try to make a little less noise, inasmuch as it was a school and people were trying to study.

It ain't fair to the others, old man Dawson said. They're trying to learn something for themselves.

We can't help it, Joey said. It hurts.

That I know, old man Dawson said, but it seems to me there's such a thing as modulation. I believe a lad can overdo his howling if he ain't thoughtful of others. Just try to modulate that awful howl a little. I think you can do it.

Then he gave Joey a strapping of twenty and Joey tried his best not to howl so loud. After the strapping his face was very red and old man Dawson was very tired.

How was that? Joey said.

That was better, old man Dawson said. By far the most courteous you've managed yet.

I did my best, Joey said.

I'm grateful to you, old man Dawson said.

He was tired and out of breath. I moved up to the chair in front of him that he furnished during these matters to help us suffer the stinging pain. I got in the right position and he said, Wait a minute, Aram. Give a man a chance to get his breath. I'm not twenty-three years old. I'm sixty-three. Let me rest a minute.

> Now the circus was back in town . . .

All right, I said, but I sure would like to get this over with.

Don't howl too loud, he said. Folks passing by in the street are liable to think this is a veritable chamber of tortures. Does it really hurt that much?

You can ask Joey, I said.

How about it, Joey? old man Dawson said. Aren't you lads exaggerating just a little? Perhaps to impress someone in your room? Some girl, perhaps?

We don't howl to impress anybody, Mr. Dawson, Joey said. We wouldn't howl if we could help it. Howling makes us feel ashamed, doesn't it, Aram?

It's awfully embarrassing to go back to our seats in our room after howling that way, I said. We'd rather not howl if we could help it.

Well, old man Dawson said, I'll not be unreasonable. I'll only ask you to try to modulate it a little.

I'll do my best, Mr. Dawson, I said. Got your breath back?

Give me just a moment longer, Aram, Mr. Dawson said.

When he got his breath back he gave me my twenty and I howled a little louder than Joey and then we went back to class. It was awfully embarrassing. Everybody was looking at us.

Well, Joey said, what did you expect? The rest of you would fall down and die if you got twenty. You wouldn't howl a little, you'd die.

That'll be enough out of you, Miss Flibety said.

Well, it's true, Joey said. They're all scared. A circus comes to town and what do they do? They come to school. They don't go out to the circus.

That'll be enough, Miss Flibety said.

Who do they think they are, giving us dirty looks? Joey said.

Miss Flibety lifted her hand, hushing Joey.

125　Now the circus was back in town, another year had gone by, it was April again, and we were on our way out to the grounds. Only this time it was worse than ever because they'd seen us at school and knew we were going out to the circus.

Do you think they'll send Stafford after us? I said.

Stafford was the truant officer.

130　We can always run, Joey said. If he comes, I'll go one way, you go another. He can't chase both of us. At least one of us will get away.

All right, I said. Suppose one of us gets caught?

Well, let's see, Joey said. Should the one who isn't caught give himself up or should he wreck Stafford's Ford?

135　I vote for wreck, I said.

So do I, Joey said, so wreck it is.

When we got out to the grounds a couple of the little tents were up, and the big one was going up. We stood around and watched. It was great the way they did it. Just a handful of guys who looked like tramps

140　doing work you'd think no less than a hundred men could do. Doing it with style, too.

All of a sudden a man everybody called Red hollered at me and Joey.

Here, you two, he said, give us a hand.

Me and Joey ran over to him.

145　Yes, sir, I said.

He was a small man with very broad shoulders and very big hands. You didn't feel that he was small, because he seemed so powerful and because he had so much thick red hair on his head. You thought he was practically a giant.

150　He handed me and Joey a rope. The rope was attached to some canvas that was lying on the ground.

This is going to be easy, Red said. As the boys lift the pole and get it in place you keep pulling the rope, so the canvas will go up with the pole.

Yes, sir, Joey said.

155　Everybody was busy when we saw Stafford.

We can't run now, I said.

Let him come, Joey said. We told Red we'd give him a hand and we're going to do it.

I'll tell you what, I said. We'll tell him we'll go with him after we get

160　the canvas up; then we'll run.

All right, Joey said.

Stafford was a big fellow in a business suit who had a beef-red face and looked as if he ought to be a lawyer or something. He came over and said, All right you hooligans, come along with me.

165　　We promised to give Red a hand, Joey said. We'll come just as soon as we get this canvas up.

We were pulling for all we were worth, slipping and falling. The men were all working hard. Red was hollering orders, and then the whole thing was over and we had done our part.

170　　We didn't even get a chance to find out what Red was going to say to us, or if he was going to invite us to sit at the table for lunch, or what.

Joey busted loose and ran one way and I ran the other and Stafford came after me. I heard the circus men laughing and Red hollering, Run, boy, run. He can't catch you. He's soft. Give him a good run. He needs 175 the exercise.

I could hear Stafford, too. He was very sore and he was cussing.

I got away, though, and stayed low until I saw him drive off in his Ford. Then I went back to the big tent and found Joey.

We'll get it this time, Joey said.

180　　I guess it'll be Reform School this time, I said.

No, Joey said. I guess it'll be thirty. We're going to do some awful howling if it is. Thirty's a lot of whacks even if he *is* sixty-three years old. He ain't exactly a weakling.

Thirty? I said. Ouch. That's liable to make me cry.

185　　Maybe, Joey said. Me too, maybe. Seems like ten can make you cry, then you hold off till it's eleven, then twelve, and you think you'll start crying on the next one, but you don't. We haven't so far, anyway. Maybe we will when it's thirty.

Oh, well, I said, that's tomorrow.

190　　Red gave us some more work to do around the grounds and let us sit next to him at lunch. It was swell. We talked to some acrobats who were Spanish, and to a family of Italians who worked with horses. We saw both shows, the afternoon one and the evening one, and then we helped with the work, taking the circus to pieces again; then we went 195 down to the trains, and then home. I got home real late. In the morning I was sleepy when I had to get up for school.

They were waiting for us. Miss Flibety didn't even let us sit down for the roll call. She just told us to go to the office. Old man Dawson was waiting for us, too. Stafford was there, too, and very sore.

200　　I figured, Well, here's where we go to Reform School.

Here they are, Mr. Dawson said to Stafford. Take them away, if you like.

It was easy to tell they'd been talking for some time and hadn't been getting along any too well. Old man Dawson seemed irritated and Stafford seemed sore at him.

205　　In *this* school, old man Dawson said, I do any punishing that's got to be done. Nobody else. I can't stop you from taking them to Reform School, though.

Stafford didn't say anything. He just left the office.

210 Well, lads, old man Dawson said. How was it?

We had lunch with them, Joey said.

Let's see now, old man Dawson said. What offense is this, the sixteenth or the seventeenth?

It ain't that many, Joey said. Must be eleven or twelve.

Well, old man Dawson said, I'm sure of one thing. This is the time
215 I'm supposed to make it thirty.

I think the next one is the one you're supposed to make thirty, Joey said.

No, Mr. Dawson said, we've lost track somewhere, but I'm sure this is the time it goes up to thirty. Who's going to be first?

Me, I said.

220 All right, Aram, Mr. Dawson said. Take a good hold on the chair, brace yourself, and try to modulate your howl.

Yes, sir, I said. I'll do my best, but thirty's an awful lot.

Well, a funny thing happened. He gave me thirty all right and I howled all right, but it was a modulated howl. It was the most modulated howl
225 I ever howled; because it was the easiest strapping I ever got. I counted them and there were thirty all right, but they didn't hurt, so I didn't cry, as I was afraid I might.

It was the same with Joey. We stood together waiting to be dismissed.

I'm awfully grateful to you boys, old man Dawson said, for modulating
230 your howls so nicely this time. I don't want people to think I'm killing you.

We wanted to thank him for giving us such easy strappings, but we couldn't say it. I think he knew the way we felt, though, because he smiled in a way that gave us an idea he knew.

Then we went back to class.

235 It was swell because we knew everything would be all right till the County Fair opened in September.

C UNDERSTANDING THE STORY

1 Reading Comprehension

Answer these questions to determine how well you understood the story:

1 Who is the narrator?
2 How does the narrator describe the circus? What are his exact words?
3 What is the name of the school Joey and Aram attend? What grade are they in?
4 In what month does the story take place?
5 Who is Mr. Stafford? Mr. Dawson?
6 Is this story humorous or sad?
7 How does Saroyan create the mood of the story? Cite examples from the story.

2 Guessing Meaning from Context

The words in the list are in the story. Find the words in the story and try to understand their meanings. Write the appropriate word(s) in each sentence. Use each word only once.

sore	reform school	modulation	tramps
irritated	liable	hooligans	truant officer
veritable	wrecked	howl	
canvas	exaggerating	hollered	

1 A(n) _truant officer_ reports students who are not in school.

2 Truant students who got into trouble used to be called _____.

3 If a teenager repeatedly commits crimes, he or she may be sent to

_____.

4 When we lower the sound of music or speaking, we use

_____.

5 His father was very _____ and _____ when Tom

_____ the car.

6 _____ is a strong fabric used to make tents and sails

for boats.

7 The fisherman was _____ when he described the size of the

fish he had caught.

8 During the Depression, many homeless people were referred to as

_____.

9 He was _____ to hear our secret, so we whispered to

each other.

10 We could hear the wind _____ through the trees as the storm

increased in intensity.

11 The city seems like a(n) _____ desert in the early morning hours.

12 Aram's mother _____ at him when she found out he had left school.

3 Grammar: Transitional Words and Phrases

When you first learned how to read, you read very short, simple sentences that helped you grasp your native language. As you became more sophisticated, your speaking and reading skills increased and you began to understand the use of transitional words and phrases. The grammar in this chapter will review the use of transitionals. By feeling comfortable using and understanding transitionals, you will become a better writer.

In "The Circus," Saroyan uses short, simple sentences because he is telling the story from the viewpoint of a young boy. However, if he had used transitional words, the effect would have been different.

Examples:
Joey and Aram wanted to go to the circus.
They left school.

These sentences could be connected with a transitional like *therefore*, as shown in these examples:

Joey and Aram wanted to go to the circus; therefore, they
    left school.
Joey and Aram wanted to go to the circus. Therefore, they left school.

Transitionals connect words and sentences to create a smoother style of writing. You should be familiar with the following transitional words:

also	furthermore	nevertheless	still
although	however	nonetheless	then
consequently	instead	otherwise	therefore
finally	meanwhile	similarly	

continued

Transitional phrases are also frequently used to connect words and sentences.

Examples:

after all	in fact	for example
as a result	in other words	on the other hand
at any rate	on the contrary	in addition

Application   Use the transitionals in the preceding lists to join the pairs of sentences that follow.

1 We trekked through the jungle for four days. We arrived at the village.

We trekked through the jungle for four days. Finally, we arrived at the village.

2 She had studied the piano for many years. She never got over her fear of playing for an audience.

_____

3 We thought we had enough money for our vacation. We ran out of cash after the first week.

_____

4 They didn't invite me. I can't go to the party with you.

_____

5 He learned French many years ago. He remembers many words.

_____

6 I walked through the city. My friend preferred to take a bus.

_____

7 The jury doubted his innocence. He was convicted.

_____

8 Before the performance began, the orchestra was practicing. The chorus was rehearsing its songs.

_____

9 Joey and Aram were afraid of Mr. Dawson. They were afraid of Mr. Stafford.

_____

10 We couldn't get tickets. We waited in line for two hours.

_____

4 Editing

Rewrite the following story using transitional words and phrases. You may work alone or with a partner. Fill in your own missing word at the end of the paragraph.

Then write another paragraph, continuing the story and the use of transitionals.

A little girl walked to her friend's house. She became tired. She was hungry. She was lost. She wasn't afraid. She had gone to her friend's house many times before. She found a compass in her pocket. She looked at the compass. It didn't help her find the path to her friend's house. It didn't help her at all. She became angry. She became sad. She looked in her pocket again. This time she found something to help her. She found a(n) _____.

D THINKING CRITICALLY

1 Discussing the Story

Discuss the following questions with a partner, in a small group, or with the whole class:

1 Why do Aram and Joey like the circus?
2 Why did Aram forget to wake up early and go to the circus with Joey?
3 How do people from the circus treat the two boys?
4 How does the principal, Mr. Dawson, deal with the boys' truancy?
5 Do you like the boys? How does the author make the boys appealing or annoying?

2 Making Inferences

Authors often write something that is intended to have more than one meaning. While you read, look for meanings that are not explicitly stated – these are inferences. Making inferences will help you enjoy the reading on a different level. The story now has deeper significance, and you will have a better understanding of it.

Read the following lines from the story. Then circle the letter of the best inference.

1 The circus was everything everything else we knew wasn't. (line 13)
   a The circus wasn't very special.
   b The circus came to town lots of times each year.
   c The circus represented the excitement the boys felt was missing from their lives.

2 I hadn't really forgotten. What I'd done was remembered. (lines 51–52)
   a Aram is afraid of what his parents will say to him.
   b Aram has to make a choice between a strapping and running off to see the circus.
   c Aram's memory isn't very good.

3 Howling makes us feel ashamed. . . . (line 105)
   a The boys take their punishment like strong men.
   b They like being beaten.
   c They cry when they are punished.

3 Analyzing the Story: Dialogue

Look back at the Literary Term on page 219. Below, look at the lines of dialogue from the story. Before each sentence, write the number of the order it should be in to tell the plot. After each sentence, write the name of the character who is speaking. The first sentence has been done for you.

_____ I had breakfast at the circus table. _____

_____ Aram Groglanian, you stay in this room. _____

_____ All right, you hooligans, come along with me. _____

_____ I don't figure I could work with lions right away. _____

_1_ The circus is in town. _____*Joey*_____

____ Well, here's where we go to Reform School. _____

____ We can't help it. It hurts. _____

____ I believe a lad can overdo his howling . . . _____

Pair Discussion   With a partner, compare what you have written. Look back at the story and check your answers. Correct any mistakes you find. Do you think the dialogue is effective in telling the story? Do you think the dialogue in this story is natural? Why or why not?

4 Writing

Read the writing ideas that follow. Your instructor may make specific assignments or ask you to choose one of these:

1 If you were the principal, how would you treat Joey and Aram? Create a dialogue between the principal (you) and the boys.
2 Did you ever want to run away from home? Pretend you are twelve years old and you join a circus. Write about what your life would be like.
3 Do the strappings stop the boys from running off to see the circus every year? Write about another way the principal might have dealt with their truancy.
4 How does Saroyan create a humorous mood? Write an essay about the humor in the story, citing the sections that make you smile as you read them.
5 In some school systems, when students break the rules, they receive physical punishments. Write about whether you agree or disagree with this type of policy.
6 The story is written as a first-person narrative. Retell the story from another character's viewpoint.

CHAPTER 15

The Warriors

ANNA LEE WALTERS

A PREPARING TO READ

1 Think Before You Read

Answer the following questions before you read the story:

1 What does the word *warrior* suggest? Can it apply to anything else besides warfare?
2 Do you know anything about the history of the Pawnee Indians? If not, look in an encyclopedia or history book.
3 What problems do you think Native Americans encounter in today's society?
4 Do you have a favorite uncle or any other male relative who has made an impression on you? In what way has he influenced you?

2 Literary Term: Local Color

Local color is the use of specific details describing the dialect, dress, customs, and scenery associated with a particular region. An example of the use of local color would be the stories of Bret Harte, who described life in America's Wild West during the period of the Gold Rush in the mid-1800s. His characters speak in "cowboy" dialect, ride horses, and often frequent saloons. Mark Twain is another American author who used local color to create the atmosphere of life along the Mississippi River. You will learn much about the Pawnee way of life when you read "The Warriors."

3 Idioms and Expressions

You will find these idioms and expressions in the story:

hobo a homeless person who travels from place to place	**had a bite to it** sharp
brave all storms face up to all problems with courage	**exploded like a fire cracker** lost his temper
stand their ground resist, never give up	**followed at his heels** followed him around all day
at the top of their lungs in a loud voice	**a vacant look** an expression that indicates a person is not functioning normally

B THE STORY

About the Author

Anna Lee Walters (born in 1946) is a Native American poet, essayist, novelist, and short story writer, as well as a publisher. She was born in Oklahoma but later moved to a Navajo reservation in Arizona, where she has devoted her life to Native American cultural affairs.

She studied at the College of Santa Fe in New Mexico and married a Navajo artist, Harry Walters. She began her literary career as a technical writer and editor at the Navajo Community College Press, where she is presently director.

All of her articles and fictional pieces deal with Native American life. She published a novel, *The Ghost Singer*, in 1988 and has published several collections of short stories over the last twenty years. Walters works tirelessly promoting Native American literature and has edited an anthology entitled *Neon Powwow: New Native American Voices of the Southwest*. For her own short stories, Walters draws from her Pawnee ancestry to create interesting tales, as you will see when you read "The Warriors."

The Warriors

In our youth, we saw hobos come and go, sliding by our faded white house like wary cats who did not want us too close. Sister and I waved at the strange procession of passing men and women hobos. Just between ourselves, Sister and I talked of that hobo parade. We guessed
5   at and imagined the places and towns we thought the hobos might have come from or had been. Mostly they were white or black people. But there were Indian hobos, too. It never occurred to Sister and me that this would be Uncle Ralph's end.

Sister and I were little, and Uncle Ralph came to visit us. He lifted
10   us over his head and shook us around him like gourd rattles. He was Momma's younger brother, and he could have disciplined us if he so desired. That was part of our custom. But he never did. Instead, he taught us Pawnee words. "*Pari* is Pawnee and *pita* is man," he said. Between the words, he tapped out drumbeats with his fingers on the table top,
15   ghost dance and round dance songs that he suddenly remembered and sang. His melodic voice lifted over us and hung around the corners of the house for days. His stories of life and death were fierce and gentle. Warriors dangled in delicate balance.

He told us his version of the story of Pahukatawa, a Skidi Pawnee
20   warrior. He was killed by the Sioux, but the animals, feeling compassion for him, brought Pahukatawa to life again. "The Evening Star and the Morning Star bore children and some people say that these offspring are who we are," he often said. At times he pointed to those stars and greeted them by their Pawnee names. He liked to pray for Sister and me,
25   for everyone and every tiny thing in the world, but we never heard him ask for anything for himself from *Atius*, the Father.

"For beauty is why we live," Uncle Ralph said when he talked of precious things only the Pawnees know. "We die for it, too." He called himself an ancient Pawnee warrior when he was quite young. He told us that warriors must brave all storms and odds and stand their ground. He knew intimate details of every battle the Pawnees ever fought since Pawnee time began, and Sister and I knew even then that Uncle Ralph had a great battlefield of his own.

As a child I thought that Uncle Ralph had been born into the wrong time. The Pawnees had been ravaged so often by then. The tribe of several thousand when it was at its peak over a century before were then a few hundred people who had been closely confined for more than a hundred years. The warrior life was gone. Uncle Ralph was trapped in a transparent bubble of a new time. The bubble bound him tight as it blew around us.

Uncle Ralph talked obsessively of warriors, painted proud warriors who shrieked poignant battle cries at the top of their lungs and died with honor. Sister and I were little then, lost from him in the world of children who saw everything with children's eyes. And though we saw with wide eyes the painted warriors that he fantasized and heard their fierce and haunting battle cries, we did not hear his. Now that we are old and Uncle Ralph has been gone for a long time, Sister and I know that when he died, he was tired and alone. But he was a warrior.

The hobos were always around in our youth. Sister and I were curious about them, and this curiosity claimed much of our time. They crept by the house at all hours of the day and night, dressed in rags and odd clothing. They wandered to us from the railroad tracks where they had leaped from slow-moving boxcars onto the flatland. They hid in high clumps of weeds and brush that ran along the fence near the tracks. The hobos usually traveled alone, but Sister and I saw them come together, like poor families, to share a can of beans or a tin of sardines that they ate with sticks or twigs. Uncle Ralph also watched them from a distance.

One early morning, Sister and I crossed the tracks on our way to school and collided with a tall, haggard white man. He wore a very old-fashioned pin-striped black jacket covered with lint and soot. There was fright in his eyes when they met ours. He scurried around us, quickening his pace. The pole over his shoulder where his possessions hung in a bundle at the end bounced as he nearly ran from us.

"Looks just like a scared jackrabbit," Sister said, watching him dart away.

That evening we told Momma about the scared man. She warned us about the dangers of hobos as our father threw us a stern look. Uncle Ralph was visiting but he didn't say anything. He stayed the night and Sister asked him, "Hey, Uncle Ralph, why do you suppose they's hobos?"

70   Uncle Ralph was a large man. He took Sister and put her on one knee. "You see, Sister," he said, "hobos are a different kind. They see things in a different way. Them hobos are kind of like us. We're not like other people in some ways and yet we are. It has to do with what you see and feel when you look at this old world."

75   His answer satisfied Sister for a while. He taught us some more Pawnee words that night.

Not long after Uncle Ralph's explanation, Sister and I surprised a black man with white whiskers and fuzzy hair. He was climbing through the barbed-wire fence that marked our property line. He wore faded

80   blue overalls with pockets stuffed full of handkerchiefs. He wiped sweat from his face. When it dried, he looked up and saw us. I remembered what Uncle Ralph had said and wondered what the black man saw when he looked at us standing there.

"We might scare him," Sister said softly to me, remembering the

85   white man who had scampered way.

Sister whispered, "Hi," to the black man. Her voice was barely audible.

"Boy, it's sure hot," he said. His voice was big and he smiled.

"Where are you going?" Sister asked.

"Me? Nowheres, I guess," he muttered.

90   "Then what you doing here?" Sister went on. She was bold for a seven-year-old kid. I was older but I was also quieter. "This here place is ours," she said.

He looked around and saw our house with its flowering mimosa trees and rich green mowed lawn stretching out before him. Other houses sat

95   around ours.

"I reckon I'm lost," he said.

Sister pointed to the weeds and brush further up the road. "That's where you want to go. That's where they all go, the hobos."

I tried to quiet Sister but she didn't hush. "The hobos stay up there,"

100 she said. "You a hobo?"

He ignored her question and asked his own. "Say, what is you all? You not black, you not white. What is you all?"

Sister looked at me. She put one hand on her chest and the other hand on me. "We Indians!" Sister said.

105 He stared at us and smiled again. "Is that a fact?" he said.

"Know what kind of Indians we are?" Sister asked him.

He shook his fuzzy head. "Indians is Indians, I guess," he said.

Sister wrinkled her forehead and retorted, "Not us! We not like others. We see things different. We're Pawnees. We're warriors!"

110 I pushed my elbow into Sister's side. She quieted.

The man was looking down the road and he shuffled his feet. "I'd best go," he said.

Sister pointed to the brush and weeds one more time. "That way," she said.

115　He climbed back through the fence and brush as Sister yelled, "Bye now!" He waved a damp handkerchief.

Sister and I didn't tell Momma and Dad about the black man. But much later Sister told Uncle Ralph every word that had been exchanged with the black man. Uncle Ralph listened and smiled.

120　Months later when the warm weather had cooled and Uncle Ralph came to stay with us for a couple of weeks, Sister and I went to the hobo place. We had planned it for a long time. That afternoon when we pushed away the weeds, not a hobo was in sight.

The ground was packed down tight in the clearing among the high

125　weeds. We walked around the encircling brush and found folded cardboards stacked together. Burned cans in assorted sizes were stashed under the cardboards, and there were remains of old fires. Rags were tied to the brush, snapping in the hard wind.

Sister said, "Maybe they're all in the boxcars now. It's starting to

130　get cold."

She was right. The November wind had a bite to it and the cold stung our hands and froze our breaths as we spoke.

"You want to go over to them boxcars?" she asked. We looked at the Railroad Crossing sign where the boxcars stood.

135　I was prepared to answer when a voice roared from somewhere behind us.

"Now, you young ones, you git on home! Go on! Git!"

A man crawled out of the weeds and looked angrily at us. His eyes were red and his face was unshaven. He wore a red plaid shirt with

140　striped gray and black pants too large for him. His face was swollen and bruised. An old woolen pink scarf hid some of the bruise marks around his neck, and his topcoat was splattered with mud.

Sister looked at him. She stood close to me and told him defiantly, "You can't tell us what to do! You don't know us!"

145　He didn't answer Sister but tried to stand. He couldn't. Sister ran to him and took his arm and pulled on it. "You need help?" she questioned.

He frowned at her but let us help him. He was tall. He seemed to be embarrassed by our help.

"You Indian, ain't you?" I dared to ask him.

150　He didn't answer me but looked at his feet as if they could talk so he wouldn't have to. His feet were in big brown overshoes.

"Who's your people?" Sister asked. He looked to be about Uncle Ralph's age when he finally lifted his face and met mine. He didn't respond for a minute. Then he sighed. "I ain't got no people," he told

155　us as he tenderly stroked his swollen jaw.

"Sure you got people. Our folks says a man's always got people," I said softly. The wind blew our clothes and covered the words.

But he heard. He exploded like a firecracker. "Well I don't! I ain't got no people! I ain't got nobody!"

"What you doing out here anyway?" Sister asked. "You hurt? You want to come over to our house?"

"Naw," he said. "Now you little ones, go on home. Don't be walking round out here. Didn't nobody tell you little girls ain't supposed to be going round by themselves? You might git hurt."

165 "We just wanted to talk to hobos," Sister said.

"Naw, you don't. Just go on home. Your folks is probably looking for you and worrying 'bout you."

I took Sister's arm and told her we were going home. Then we said bye to the man. But Sister couldn't resist a few last words, "You Indian, 170 ain't you?"

He nodded his head like it was a painful thing to do. "Yeah, I'm Indian."

"You ought to go on home yourself," Sister said. "Your folks probably looking for you and worrying 'bout you."

His voice rose again as Sister and I walked away from him. "I told 175 you kids, I don't have no people!" There was exasperation in his voice.

Sister would not be outdone. She turned and yelled, "Oh yeah? You Indian ain't you? Ain't you?" she screamed. "We your people!"

His topcoat and pink scarf flapped in the wind as we turned away from him.

180 We went home to Momma and Dad and Uncle Ralph then. Uncle Ralph met us at the front door. "Where you all been?" he asked looking toward the railroad tracks. Momma and Dad were talking in the kitchen.

"Just playing, Uncle," Sister and I said simultaneously.

Uncle Ralph grabbed both Sister and me by our hands and yanked us 185 out the door. "*Awkuh!*" he said, using the Pawnee expression to show his dissatisfaction.

Outside, we sat on the cement porch. Uncle Ralph was quiet for a long time, and neither Sister nor I knew what to expect.

"I want to tell you all a story," he finally said. "Once, there were 190 these two rats who ran around everywhere and got into everything all the time. Everything they were told not to do, well they went right out and did. They'd get into one mess and then another. It seems that they never could learn."

At that point Uncle Ralph cleared his throat. He looked at me and said, 195 "Sister, do you understand this story? Is it too hard for you? You're older."

I nodded my head up and down and said, "I understand."

Then Uncle Ralph looked at Sister. He said to her, "Sister, do I need to go on with this story?"

Sister shook her head from side to side. "Naw, Uncle Ralph," she said.

200 "So you both know how this story ends?" he said gruffly. Sister and I bobbed our heads up and down again.

We followed at his heels the rest of the day. When he tightened the loose hide on top of his drum, we watched him and held it in place as

he laced the wet hide down. He got his drumsticks down from the top
205 shelf of the closet and began to pound the drum slowly.

"Where you going, Uncle Ralph?" I asked. Sister and I knew that
when he took his drum out, he was always gone shortly after.

"I have to be a drummer at some doings tomorrow," he said.

"You a good singer, Uncle Ralph," Sister said. "You know all them
210 old songs."

"The young people nowadays, it seems they don't care 'bout nothing
that's old. They just want to go to the Moon." He was drumming low
as he spoke.

"We care, Uncle Ralph," Sister said.

215 "Why?" Uncle Ralph asked in a hard, challenging tone that he seldom
used on us.

Sister thought for a moment and then said, "I guess because you care
so much, Uncle Ralph."

His eyes softened as he said, "I'll sing you an *Eruska* song, a song
220 for the warriors."

The song he sang was a war dance song. At first Sister and I listened
attentively, but then Sister began to dance the men's dance. She had
never danced before and tried to imitate what she had seen. Her chubby
body whirled and jumped the way she'd seen the men dance. Her head
225 tilted from side to side the way the men moved theirs. I laughed aloud
at her clumsy effort, and Uncle Ralph laughed heartily, too.

Uncle Ralph went in and out of our lives after that. We heard that he
sang at one place and then another, and people came to Momma to find
him. They said that he was only one of a few who knew the old ways
230 and the songs.

When he came to visit us, he always brought something to eat.
The Pawnee custom was that the man, the warrior, should bring food,
preferably meat. Then, whatever food was brought to the host was
prepared and served to the man, the warrior, along with the host's
235 family. Many times Momma and I, or Sister and I, came home to an
empty house to find a sack of food on the table. Momma or I cooked it
for the next meal, and Uncle Ralph showed up to eat.

As Sister and I grew older, our fascination with the hobos decreased.
Other things took our time, and Uncle Ralph did not appear as frequently
240 as he did before.

Once while I was home alone, I picked up Momma's old photo album.
Inside was a gray photo of Uncle Ralph in an army uniform. Behind him
were tents on a flat terrain. Other photos showed other poses but only
in one picture did he smile. All the photos were written over in black
245 ink in Momma's handwriting. "Ralphie in Korea," the writing said.

Other photos in the album showed our Pawnee relatives. Dad was
from another tribe. Momma's momma was in the album, a tiny gray-

haired woman who no longer lived. And Momma's momma's dad was in the album; he wore old Pawnee leggings and the long feathers of a dark bird sat upon his head. I closed the album when Momma, Dad, and Sister came home.

Momma went into the kitchen to cook. She called me and Sister to help. As she put on a bibbed apron, she said, "We just came from town, and we saw someone from home there." She meant someone from her tribal community.

"This man told me that Ralphie's been drinking hard," she said sadly. "He used to do that quite a bit a long time ago, but we thought it had stopped. He seemed to be all right for a few years." We cooked and then ate in silence.

Washing the dishes, I asked Momma, "How come Uncle Ralph never did marry?"

Momma looked up at me but was not surprised by my question. She answered, "I don't know, Sister. It would have been better if he had. There was one woman who I thought he really loved. I think he still does. I think it had something to do with Mom. She wanted him to wait."

"Wait for what?" I asked.

"I don't know," Momma said, and sank into a chair.

After that we heard unsettling rumors of Uncle Ralph drinking here and there.

He finally came to the house once when only I happened to be home. He was haggard and tired. His appearance was much like that of the white man that Sister and I met on the railroad tracks years before.

I opened the door when he tapped on it. Uncle Ralph looked years older than his age. He brought food in his arms. "*Nowa*, Sister," he said in greeting. "Where's the other one?" He meant my sister.

"She's gone now, Uncle Ralph. School in Kansas," I answered. "Where you been, Uncle Ralph? We been worrying about you."

He ignored my question and said, "I bring food. The warrior brings home food. To his family, to his people." His face was lined and had not been cleaned for days. He smelled of cheap wine.

I asked again, "Where you been, Uncle Ralph?"

He forced himself to smile. "Pumpkin Flower," he said, using the Pawnee name, "I've been out with my warriors all this time."

He put one arm around me as we went to the kitchen table with the food. "That's what your Pawnee name is. Now don't forget it."

"Did somebody bring you here, Uncle Ralph, or are you on foot?" I asked him.

"I'm on foot," he answered. "Where's your Momma?"

I told him that she and Dad would be back soon. I started to prepare the food he brought.

Then I heard Uncle Ralph say, "Life is sure hard sometimes. Sometimes it seems I just can't go on."

"What's wrong, Uncle Ralph?" I asked.

Uncle Ralph let out a bitter little laugh. "What's wrong?" he repeated. "What's wrong? All my life, I've tried to live what I've been taught, but Pumpkin Flower, some things are all wrong!"

He took a folded pack of Camel cigarettes from his coat pocket. His hand shook as he pulled one from the pack and lit the end. "Too much drink," he said sadly. "That stuff is bad for us."

"What are you trying to do, Uncle Ralph?" I asked him.

"Live," he said.

He puffed on the shaking cigarette a while and said, "The old people said to live beautifully with prayers and song. Some died for beauty, too."

"How do we do that, Uncle Ralph, live for beauty?" I asked.

"It's simple, Pumpkin Flower," he said. "Believe!"

"Believe what?" I asked.

He looked at me hard. "*Awkuh!*" he said. "That's one of the things that is wrong. Everyone questions. Everyone doubts. No one believes in the old ways anymore. They want to believe when it's convenient, when it doesn't cost them anything and they get something in return. There are no more believers. There are no more warriors. They are all gone. Those who are left only want to go to the Moon."

A car drove up outside. It was Momma and Dad. Uncle Ralph heard it too. He slumped in the chair, resigned to whatever Momma would say to him.

Momma came in first. Dad then greeted Uncle Ralph and disappeared into the back of the house. Custom and etiquette required that Dad, who was not a member of Momma's tribe, allow Momma to handle her brother's problems.

She hugged Uncle Ralph. Her eyes filled with tears when she saw how thin he was and how his hands shook.

"Ralphie," she said, "you look awful, but I am glad to see you."

She then spoke to him of everyday things, how the car failed to start and the latest gossip. He was silent, tolerant of the passing of time in this way. His eyes sent me a pleading look while his hands shook and he tried to hold them still.

When supper was ready, Uncle Ralph went to wash himself for the meal. When he returned to the table, he was calm. His hands didn't shake so much.

At first he ate without many words, but in the course of the meal he left the table twice. Each time he came back, he was more talkative than before, answering Momma's questions in Pawnee. He left the table a third time and Dad rose.

Dad said to Momma, "He's drinking again. Can't you tell?" Dad left the table and went outside.

Momma frowned. A determined look grew on her face.

When Uncle Ralph sat down to the table once more, Momma told him, "Ralphie, you're my brother but I want you to leave now. Come back when you're sober."

He held a tarnished spoon in midair and put it down slowly. He hadn't finished eating, but he didn't seem to mind leaving. He stood, looked at me with his red eyes, and went to the door. Momma followed him. In a low voice she said, "Ralphie, you've got to stop drinking and wandering – or don't come to see us again."

He pulled himself to his full height then. His frame filled the doorway. He leaned over Momma and yelled, "Who are you? Are you God that you will say what will be or will not be?"

Momma met his angry eyes. She stood firm and did not back down.

His eyes finally dropped from her face to the linoleum floor. A cough came from deep in his throat.

"I'll leave here," he said. "But I'll get all my warriors and come back! I have thousands of warriors and they'll ride with me. We'll get our bows and arrows. Then we'll come back!" He staggered out the door.

In the years that followed, Uncle Ralph saw us only when he was sober. He visited less and less. When he did show up, he did a tapping ritual on our front door. We welcomed the rare visits. Occasionally he stayed at our house for a few days at a time when he was not drinking. He slept on the floor.

He did odd jobs for minimum pay but never complained about the work or money. He'd acquired a vacant look in his eyes. It was the same look that Sister and I had seen in the hobos when we were children. He wore a similar careless array of clothing and carried no property with him at all.

The last time he came to the house, he called me by my English name and asked if I remembered anything of all that he'd taught me. His hair had turned pure white. He looked older than anyone I knew. I marveled at his appearance and said, "I remember everything." That night I pointed out his stars for him and told him how Pahukatawa lived and died and lived again through another's dreams. I'd grown, and Uncle Ralph could not hold me on his knee anymore. His arm circled my waist while we sat on the grass.

He was moved by my recitation and clutched my hand tightly. He said, "It's more than this. It's more than just repeating words. You know that, don't you?"

I nodded my head. "Yes, I know. The recitation is the easiest part but it's more than this, Uncle Ralph."

He was quiet, but after a few minutes his hand touched my shoulder. He said, "I couldn't make it work. I tried to fit the pieces."

"I know," I said.

"Now before I go," he said, "do you know who you are?"

The question took me by surprise. I thought very hard. I cleared my throat and told him, "I know that I am fourteen. I know that it's too young."

"Do you know that you are a Pawnee?" he asked in a choked whisper.

"Yes, Uncle," I said.

"Good," he said with a long sigh that was swallowed by the night.

Then he stood and said, "Well, Sister, I have to go. Have to move on."

"Where are you going?" I asked. "Where all the warriors go?" I teased.

He managed a smile and a soft laugh. "Yeah, wherever the warriors are, I'll find them."

I said to him, "Before you go, I want to ask you . . . Uncle Ralph, can women be warriors too?"

He laughed again and hugged me merrily. "Don't tell me you want to be one of the warriors too?"

"No, Uncle," I said. "Just one of yours." I hated to let him go because I knew I would not see him again.

He pulled away. His last words were, "Don't forget what I've told you all these years. It's the only chance not to become what everyone else is. Do you understand?"

I nodded and he left.

I never saw him again.

The years passed quickly. I moved away from Momma and Dad and married. Sister left before I did.

Years later in another town, hundreds of miles away, I awoke in a terrible gloom, a sense that something was gone from the world the Pawnees knew. The despair filled days, though the reason for the sense of loss went unexplained. Finally, the telephone rang. Momma was on the line. She said, "Sister came home for a few days not too long ago. While she was here and alone, someone tapped on the door, like Ralphie always does. Sister yelled, 'Is that you, Uncle Ralphie? Come on in.' But no one entered."

Then I understood that Uncle Ralph was dead. Momma probably knew too. She wept softly into the phone.

Later Momma received an official call confirming Uncle Ralph's death. He had died from exposure in a hobo shanty, near the railroad tracks outside a tiny Oklahoma town. He'd been dead for several days and nobody knew but Momma, Sister, and me.

Momma reported to me that the funeral was well attended by the Pawnee people. Uncle Ralph and I had said our farewells years earlier. Momma told me that someone there had spoken well of Uncle Ralph before they put him in the ground. It was said that "Ralphie came from a fine family, an old line of warriors."

C UNDERSTANDING THE STORY

1 Reading Comprehension

Answer these questions to determine how well you understood the story:

1 Why did the children enjoy Uncle Ralph's visits?
2 What were some of the things he taught them?
3 Why were the narrator and her sister fascinated with hobos? What connection do the hobos have to the rest of the story?
4 What was Uncle Ralph's problem?
5 How did the narrator, her sister, and her mother know that Uncle Ralph was dead even before they received an official call reporting his death?

2 Guessing Meaning from Context

The words in the list are in the story. Find the words in the story and try to understand their meanings. Then write the appropriate word(s) in each sentence. Use each word only once.

wary	obsessively	haggard	etiquette
gourd	poignant	exasperation	array
melodic	fantasized	rumors	offspring
ravage	collided	unsettling	

1 The weary mother had her hands full taking care of six noisy

_____offspring_____ .

2 When the soldier returned from battle and saw his child for the first time,

it was a(n) _____ scene.

3 Books of _____ indicate that gifts should be acknowledged

with a letter of appreciation.

4 During the American Civil War, General Sherman, a Yankee commander,

ordered his troops to _____ the countryside and burn Atlanta.

5 Uncle Ralph _____ about bringing thousands of warriors to

avenge the insults he felt he had received.

6 Uncle Ralph spoke _____ of the warriors and his Pawnee heritage.

7 The children were enchanted with the _____ of toys they saw in the shop window.

8 In the summer, people should be _____ of ticks, especially in wooded areas.

9 The two cars _____ with each other when they both tried to pass on the highway.

10 The Indians made a drinking cup from the rind of a plant, which they call a(n) _____.

11 After Uncle Ralph had been drinking, he looked ill and _____.

12 Uncle Ralph had a(n) _____ voice when he sang Pawnee songs.

13 We left the restaurant in _____ because the service was so bad.

14 Nobody should listen to _____ , which are seldom based on fact.

15 The _____ news greatly disturbed us.

3 Grammar: Using Commas, Semicolons, and Colons

Punctuation helps the reader better understand what you are writing. This final grammar exercise will help you edit your own writing on tests and in essays. By following the exercises below, you will gain more confidence in making your thoughts and ideas clear to whoever reads them.

continued

As you read "The Warriors," you probably noticed sentences like this: "He told us his version of the story of Pahukatawa, a Skidi Pawnee warrior." Why does the author place a comma after the word *Pahukatawa?* Immediately following Pahukatawa is the identification of the name, "a Skidi Pawnee warrior." This construction is called an appositive – it identifies or describes the word preceding it.

You must use a comma to separate the identification from the noun or pronoun it describes. Otherwise, the meaning would be obscure.

Example:
Uncle Ralph our Pawnee relative is here.

The reader could interpret this sentence in either of two ways:

1. Uncle Ralph is being told that a Pawnee relative has arrived. If so, the proper punctuation is: Uncle Ralph, our Pawnee relative is here. This is called direct address because the speaker is talking *to* Uncle Ralph, not *about* him.
2. Uncle Ralph *is* the Pawnee relative. In this instance, the sentence must be written with commas before and after "our Pawnee relative": Uncle Ralph, our Pawnee relative, is here. This construction shows an appositive.

You have now learned two uses of the comma: before or after direct address, and to separate an appositive from the word it modifies.

Examples:
Have you written this letter, Maria? (direct address)
Maria, our secretary, has written the letter. (appositive)

The comma is also used to separate items in a series. Suppose you go to the store to buy groceries. You must separate one item from another with a comma.

Example:
I bought coffee, tea, peaches, pears, and a dozen eggs. (series)

Another use of the comma is after an introductory clause. This means the clause must come at the beginning of the sentence.

Example:
Because Uncle Ralph was proud of his heritage, he told the children Pawnee stories. (introductory clause)

The clause in color introduces the main part of the sentence and thus is followed by a comma. If the clause comes after the main part of the sentence, do not use a comma. Let's reverse the sentence:

Uncle Ralph told the children Pawnee stories because he was proud of his heritage.

The conjunction *because* directly connects the two clauses into one sentence, and no comma is used.

Commas separate parenthetical expressions from the rest of the sentence. A parenthetical expression is extra information that could be omitted. If a parenthetical expression is left out, the sentence still makes sense:

> The narrator of the story**, as well as her sister,** listened attentively to Uncle Ralph's tales of the Pawnees. (parenthetical expression)

The expression, "as well as her sister," adds information. It is separated by commas because it could be lifted out of the sentence. The narrator is the subject, not her sister. Phrases like *as well as*, *together with*, and *including* introduce parenthetical expressions.

If you look at the dialogue in the story "The Warriors," you will see that commas are used before or after direct quotations. The sentences are punctuated as follows:

> Uncle Ralph was a large man. He took Sister and put her on one knee. "You see, Sister," he said, "hobos are a different kind. They see things in a different way."

Notice that the comma goes inside the quotation marks except when the quotation resumes after the word *said*. Then the comma comes after the word *said* and before the quotation.

For each change of speaker, the author begins a new paragraph, as shown in the following sentences. In the last sentence, note that a question mark is used instead of a comma.

> Sister whispered, "Hi," to the black man. Her voice was barely audible.

> "Boy, it's sure hot," he said. His voice was big and he smiled.
> "Where are you going?" Sister asked.

continued

Commas are also used to set off addresses and complete dates:

Chicago, Illinois   June 5, 1995

Do not use a comma to separate a partial date, such as June 5.

Commas often set off transitional or introductory words from the rest of the sentence. These words include *of course, for instance, however, therefore, indeed, yes,* and *no.*

Examples:
You are, **of course**, going to the meeting. (transitional words)
Yes, we are thoroughly prepared to make the report.
(introductory word)

Finally, commas may be used to separate a nonrestrictive clause from the rest of the sentence. Nonrestrictive simply means not necessary.

Example:
Helen Smith, **who is my sister,** is the president of our club.
(nonrestrictive)

The clause "who is my sister" is not necessary to identify or describe Helen Smith. Like a parenthetical expression, it is used to give extra information. Therefore, you can omit it if you choose. In the following sentence, however, you need the clause to complete the meaning:

The woman who is wearing a blue suit is Helen Smith. (restrictive)

The clause "who is wearing a blue suit" is essential to the meaning of the sentence. This is a restrictive clause (necessary) and it cannot be omitted; therefore, no commas are used.

The comma, which you have just studied, could be called a half-stop. It does not, by itself, join complete sentences. If you wish to join two short sentences, you should use either a conjunction or a semicolon [;], which is a full stop.

Examples:
It was the best of times **but** it was the worst of times.
It was the best of times; it was the worst of times.
Mary is a physician *and* her brother studies law.
Mary is a physician; her brother studies law.

The semicolon is also used to separate complicated items in a series:

> On our trip we visited London, England; Paris, France; Vienna, Austria; and Rome, Italy.

If you used only commas, the same sentence would look like this:

> On our trip we visited London, England, Paris, France, Vienna, Austria, and Rome, Italy.

Unless you use the semicolon, the same sentence looks as if the travelers visited eight places, not four.

The semicolon is also used before the following words in a compound sentence: *however, therefore, nevertheless,* and *whereas.* Remember: These words are not conjunctions; their sole function is to introduce an idea.

Examples:
We received your order for twelve laser printers; **however,** we do not carry the model you requested. (two complete sentences)
I am going home for the holidays; **therefore,** I must pack my luggage. (two complete sentences)

The colon [:] is used before a long quotation or a long list of items, especially after the word *following* or the expression *as follows.*

Examples:
John Adams, the second president of the United States, wrote: "Yesterday the greatest question was decided whichever was debated in America; and a greater perhaps never was nor will be, decided among men. A resolution was passed without one dissenting colony that these United Colonies are free and independent states."
Please send the **following** school supplies: 10 packages of 8 X 11 lined notebook paper, 100 number 2 pencils, 5 loose-leaf notebooks with soft covers, and 6 boxes of white chalk.

The colon is also used to express the exact time.

Example:
We are leaving at 8:20 p.m.

Application   Insert the necessary commas, question marks, and quotation marks in each of the following sentences:

1 Uncle Ralph asked , "Do you know what hobos are ?"

2 Because Indians live on reservations they often are isolated from townspeople.

3 Phoenix Arizona is located in the West.

4 On July 4 1776 the Declaration of Independence was signed.

5 The narrator as well as her sister was fascinated with hobos.

6 Uncle Ralph who was a Pawnee told his nieces many Indian stories.

7 Have you read asked the teacher many stories about Indian tribes.

8 George Washington the first president of the United States is called the father of our country.

9 My dog an Irish setter likes to run through the woods.

10 When you go to the market please buy some pears apples and grapes.

11 Indeed I shall come to your party on Thursday.

12 We are of course expecting you.

13 Anna Lee Walters the author of this story is a Native American.

14 Although we had planned for twenty guests more than thirty people arrived.

4 Editing

Punctuate the following paragraph:

After we came to the United States we decided to plan a trip to the West. We want to visit the following places Denver Colorado Phoenix Arizona Santa Fe New Mexico Salt Lake City Utah and the national parks. We also want to see the Indian reservations particularly the Pawnees. We read about them in the stories of Anna Lee Walters a Native American author. She is a writer she is an educator As a Native American she knows many interesting tales.

My friend Fran told me Don't miss the Grand Canyon it is an incredible sight. Indeed we look forward to our trip across the United States.

D THINKING CRITICALLY

1 Discussing the Story

Discuss the following questions with a partner, in a small group, or with the whole class:

1 What did the word *warrior* mean to Uncle Ralph? In what way was he a warrior? What was his battle?
2 What did the word *warrior* mean to the narrator and her sister when they were children? How did their concept of the term change when they grew up?
3 Why does the author introduce hobos into the story? Is there any foreshadowing in the seemingly unrelated incidents with hobos? Explain.
4 Uncle Ralph's sense of values seemed to be summed up in his statement, "For beauty is why we live." Do you agree? Or do you have a different belief about the purpose of life? Discuss.
5 Do you think that Ralph's sister was not supportive of her brother? Debate this with a partner.
6 What was Uncle Ralph's legacy to his nieces?

2 Making Inferences

> Authors often write something that is intended to have more than one meaning. While you read, look for meanings that are not explicitly stated – these are inferences. Making inferences will help you enjoy the reading on a different level. The story now has deeper significance, and you will have a better understanding of it.

Read the following lines from the story. Then circle the letter of the best inference.

1 His melodic voice lifted over us and hung around the corners of the house for days. (lines 16–17)
   a Uncle Ralph loved to sing.
   b Uncle Ralph sings because he's happy with his life.
   c Uncle Ralph has a big influence on the two girls.

2 . . . Sister and I knew even then that Uncle Ralph had a great battlefield of his own. (lines 32–33)
   a The sisters see Ralph as a Pawnee Warrior.
   b Uncle Ralph is fighting alcoholism and an inability to fit into modern society.
   c The sisters hope Uncle Ralph will become happy.

3 "I couldn't make it work. I tried to fit the pieces." (line 378)

   a Uncle Ralph is a failure.

   b Uncle Ralph learns to like the modern world.

   c Uncle Ralph couldn't adjust to the modern world.

3 Analyzing the Story: Local Color

Look back at the Literary Term on page 233. The author includes many details of the Pawnee life, which add local color to the story. Read the story again, and complete the chart below with examples of customs and beliefs that help the reader to know the Pawnee culture better.

CUSTOMS	BELIEFS
He was Momma's younger brother, and he could have disciplined us if he so desired. (lines 10–12)	"The Evening Star and the Morning Star bore children and some people say that these offspring are who we are." (lines 21–23)

Pair Discussion With a partner, compare what you have written. Correct any mistakes you find. Do you think Uncle Ralph captures the glory of the Pawnee people?

4 Writing

Read the writing ideas that follow. Your instructor may make specific assignments or ask you to choose one of these:

1 There are many Native American legends from various tribes like the Pawnees or Navajos. Look up an Indian legend and retell it in an essay.
2 Write a myth, legend, or fable from your own native culture.
3 Make up an original legend and write it as though you were Uncle Ralph telling it to his nieces.
4 The narrator says of her uncle, "Uncle Ralph had been born into the wrong time." If you are familiar with the story *Don Quixote* by Cervantes, compare Uncle Ralph to Don Quixote as tragic figures living in the past.
5 Why do you suppose alcoholism afflicts some Native Americans? Do some research on the social conditions of Native Americans living on reservations and write a report of your findings.

A TAKE A CLOSER LOOK

1 Analyzing and Comparing

In each of the following sections, you are asked to think about and compare two of the stories in Part Five.

"A Rice Sandwich" and "The Circus"

- Compare Joey and Aram to Esperanza. How are their personalities different?
- Imagine that they are all in the same class. What would Esperanza learn from them? What would Joey and Aram learn from Esperanza?

"The Warriors" and "A Rice Sandwich"

- Esperanza has a dream of eating in the canteen. Uncle Ralph wants to restore the glory of his people. Compare how they each deal with disappointment when their dreams are shattered.
- If Esperanza met Uncle Ralph, what kind of advice would she give him? What advice would Ralph give Esperanza?

"The Warriors" and "The Circus"

- Imagine the sisters in "The Warriors" meet Joey and Aram from "The Circus." Do you think they would be friends? Why?
- What advice would Joey and Aram give to the sisters about their Uncle Ralph?

2 Freewriting

What was the biggest challenge you ever had to face? How did you meet this challenge? Were you successful? When you encounter new challenges, do you remember previous successes? Write the word *challenges* on a piece of paper. Now write any words you associate with the word *challenges*. Write for fifteen minutes about challenges in your own life.

B WORDS FREQUENTLY CONFUSED

Look up the meanings of the following groups of words. After you have found the meanings of these words, make up a story using at least fifteen words from this list.

Words that have similar spellings, meanings, or pronunciations are often confused with one another.

From "The Rice Sandwich"

wear (verb), ware (noun), where (adverb)

one (pronoun), won (verb)

ate (verb), eight (adjective), eighth (adverb, adjective, or noun)

tired (adjective), tried (verb)

made (verb), maid (noun)

From "The Circus"

need (noun or verb), knead (verb)

whole (adjective), hole (noun)

tear (noun), tear (verb)

fair (adjective or noun), fare (noun)

pole (noun), poll (noun or verb)

seem (verb), seam (noun)

real (adjective), reel (noun or verb)

From "The Warriors"

wary (adjective), weary (adjective)

stars (noun), stairs (noun)

brought (verb), bought (verb)

tape (noun or verb), tap (noun or verb)

Plurals of Nouns Ending in *o*

The children in "The Warriors" regarded Uncle Ralph as a *hero*. How do we make this noun plural? Nouns that end in *o* form their plurals by adding *-es* if the *o* is preceded by a consonant. Since the letter *r* is a consonant, *hero* becomes *heroes*; and *echo* is pluralized as *echoes*.

However, if a noun ending in *o* is preceded by a vowel, its plural is formed by just adding *-s*. Thus, *radio* becomes *radios*; *shampoo* becomes *shampoos*.

This pattern does *not* apply to musical terms, such as *solo*. Regardless of the letter preceding the *o*, the plural of a musical term is always formed with an *s*. Therefore, *solo* becomes *solos* in the plural, and *soprano* becomes *sopranos*.

To review these patterns, form the plural of each of the following nouns:

patio _____   basso _____

potato _____   tomato _____

studio _____   trio _____

kangaroo _____   zoo _____

stereo _____   piano _____

D FINAL REVIEW TEST

Some of the following sentences are correct; in others, there are errors in grammar or usage. If you think the sentence is correct, write the letter *C* in the space below each sentence. If the sentence is incorrect, underline the error(s) and rewrite the sentence correctly. In some instances, you may just be improving awkward constructions.

1 I like the fruit very much. I always keep it at my refrigerator.

_____

2 The store is closed. We should have went earlier.

_____

3 Not one of these stories is boring.

_____

4 We're always interesting in reading new fiction.

_____

5 Let's keep the money for ourself.

_____

6 We enjoy reading short stories by American authors.

_____

7 Each of the actors come from my home town.

_____

8 Jane and myself are going to the game.

_____

9 Here is a sample of two new pens for you to try.

_____

10 We go never to the beach on weekends. It's too crowded.

_____

11 I don't want to go with John. He drives too quick.

_____

12 The news of her unexpected marriage were surprising.

_____

13 You look tired. Don't you feel well today?

_____

14 Not one of them write a clear memo.

_____

15 There were a novel and a biography on her desk.

_____

16 That's my coat. Is this one your?

_____

17 It's too bad our dog hurt it's paw.

_____

18 If I was you, I would rent a house instead of buying one.

_____

19 We were so thirsty that we could have drank a pitcher of water.

_____

20 It was Mr. Behrman who Johnsy owed her life to.

_____

21 Ted sent flowers to my mother and I.

_____

22 The life on a farm is very difficult, especially in winter.

_____

23 Please put the milk in the refrigerator on the top shelf.

_____

24 We read often articles about life in various parts of United States.

_____

 WEBQUEST

Find more information about the topics in Part Five by going on the Internet. Go to www.cambridge.org/discoveringfiction/wq and follow the instructions for doing a WebQuest. Have fun. Enjoy the quest!

APPENDIX

The list on the left shows common errors many students make. Correct versions are on the right.

STOP: DON'T USE THESE	GO: DO USE THESE
almost people	most people
an all piece	a whole piece
arrive to New York	arrive in New York
between you and I	between you and me
enjoy to go	enjoy going
explain me	explain to me
fell off of the bus	fell off the bus
he wish, she wish	he wishes, she wishes
how you say	how do you say
if I was	if I were
I see never him	I never see him
make my homework	do my homework
more prettier	prettier
one of my friend	one of my friends
people is	people are
some persons	some people
the life is funny	life is funny
to talked	to talk
United States	the United States
want shopping	want to shop

Allegory a story with characters and actions that symbolize ideas and morals, e.g., "The Lottery"

Antagonist a character or force of nature that opposes the main character, e.g., the children in "All Summer in a Day" who keep Margot from seeing the sun

Atmosphere mood of a story created by its setting, e.g., "All Summer in a Day"

Characterization a technique the author uses to create a believable character, e.g., Mary in "Too Soon a Woman"

Climax the high point or turning point of a story, e.g., when Sue lifts the shade in "The Last Leaf "

Conflict the struggle between opposing forces, e.g., "A Visit to Grandmother"

Dialect the manner of speech used by characters to reflect their ethnic or regional background, e.g., "Thank You, Ma'm" and "The Warriors"

Dialogue the conversation carried on by characters, e.g., "The Circus"

Fable a short story that uses animals as characters to teach a lesson or moral, e.g., the story Uncle Ralph began to tell about the rats in "The Warriors"

Fantasy a story that is deliberately unreal, like a fairy tale or science fiction, e.g., "All Summer in a Day"

First Person Narrator the protagonist tells the story, e.g., "The Rice Sandwich"

Flashback a device in which the author interrupts the sequence of events to relate an earlier scene, e.g., the beginning of "Désirée's Baby"

Foreshadowing hints or clues that indicate something is about to happen, e.g., "The Lottery"

Imagery descriptive language used to paint a vivid picture of a scene, e.g., "It's a wonderful town with big old frame houses and tremendous trees whose branches meet overhead and roof the streets." (from "The Third Level")

Irony the opposite of what was intended; a cruel twist of fate, e.g., "All Summer in a Day"

Local color details of dress, speech, or customs that give the time and place of a story, e.g., "The Warriors"

Metaphor a comparison between two unlike objects to create an image, e.g., "I think the sun is a flower that blooms for just one hour." (from "All Summer in a Day")

Narrative a series of events that make up a plot

Personification giving human characteristics to an inanimate object, e.g., "Pneumonia stalked about the colony touching one here and there with his icy fingers." (from "The Last Leaf")

Plot the plan or arrangement of events that make up a story

Poetic justice the rewarding or punishing of characters in an ironic way, e.g., in "Too Soon a Woman," Mary is rewarded for her courage.

Point of view seeing the events of a story through the eyes of one or more characters, e.g., "A Day's Wait"

Protagonist the main character; the hero or heroine of a story, e.g., Charley in "The Third Level"

Realism life presented as it really is, e.g., "The Circuit" portrays the hard life of the migrant workers

Romanticism life presented as one would like it to be, as in stories with a happy ending, e.g., "The Circus"

Satire the use of ridicule or sarcasm to expose a social evil, e.g., "The One Day War"

Sense impressions a form of imagery in which the author uses language to appeal to the five senses, e.g., "An old, old ivy vine, gnarled and decayed at the root climbed half way up the brick wall. The cold breath of autumn had stricken its leaves from the vine." (from "The Last Leaf")

Setting the time or place in which a story takes place, e.g., nineteenth century Creole society in "Désirée's Baby"

Simile a comparison between unlike objects using the words *like* or *as*, e.g., "The passion that awoke in him when he saw her at the gate, swept along like an avalanche or a prairie fire." (from "Desiree's Baby")

Suspense a series of events that create tension or excitement leading to a climax, e.g., the gathering of stones and the black box in "The Lottery"

Symbolism a person, place, or object that represents an idea, e.g., the blood transfusion is a symbol of the brother's love for his sister in "Thicker than Water"

Theme the general message or idea that the author wishes to convey, e.g., the importance of Native American heritage in "The Warriors"

Tragedy the final defeat of the protagonist by the opposing forces, e.g., "Désirée's Baby"

Irregular Verbs

Verb	Past Tense	Past Participle (use with *has*, *have*, and *had*)
awake	awoke, awaked	awoken, awoke
be (am, is, are)	was (were)	been
bear	bore	borne
beat	beat	beaten, beat
become	became	become
begin	began	begun
bet	bet	bet
bite	bit	bitten
blow	blew	blown
break	broke	broken
bring	brought	brought
build	built	built
burst	burst	burst
catch	caught	caught
choose	chose	chosen
cling	clung	clung
come	came	come
cost	cost	cost
creep	crept	crept
cut	cut	cut
dive	dived, dove	dived, dove
do	did	done
draw	drew	drawn
dream	dreamt, dreamed	dreamt, dreamed
drink	drank	drunk
drive	drove	driven
eat	ate	eaten
fall	fell	fallen
feel	felt	felt
fight	fought	fought
fling	flung	flung
fly	flew	flown
forget	forgot	forgotten
freeze	froze	frozen
get	got	got, gotten
give	gave	given
go	went	gone

Verb	Past Tense	Past Participle
grow	grew	grown
hang	hung	hung
hang (a person, kill)	hanged, hung	hanged, hung
hear	heard	heard
hit	hit	hit
hurt	hurt	hurt
keep	kept	kept
know	knew	known
lay	laid	laid
lead	led	led
leave	left	left
let	let	let
lie (position)	lay	lain
lose	lost	lost
make	made	made
pay	paid	paid
put	put	put
read	read (pronounced *red*)	read (pronounced *red*)
ride	rode	ridden
ring	rang	rung
rise	rose	risen
run	ran	run
say	said	said
see	saw	seen
send	sent	sent
set	set	set
shake	shook	shaken
shine	shone	shone
show	showed	shown, showed
sing	sang	sung
sink	sank	sunk
sit	sat	sat
sleep	slept	slept
slide	slid	slid
speak	spoke	spoken
spring	sprang	sprung
steal	stole	stolen
swear	swore	sworn
swim	swam	swum

Verb	Past Tense	Past Participle
swing	swung	swung
take	took	taken
teach	taught	taught
tear	tore	torn
tell	told	told
think	thought	thought
throw	threw	thrown
wake	woke	woken
wear	wore	worn
win	won	won
write	wrote	written

ACKNOWLEDGMENTS

"A Day's Wait" by Ernest Hemingway. Reprinted with the permission of Scribner, a Division of Simon & Schuster, Inc. and The Random House Group Limited, from *Winner Take Nothing* by Ernest Hemingway. Published by Jonathan Cape. Copyright © 1933 by Charles Scribner's Sons. Copyright renewed 1961 by Mary Hemingway. All rights reserved.

"Thank You, M'am" by Langston Hughes, from *Short Stories* by Langston Hughes. First published in the Langston Hughes Reader, 1958. Copyright © 1996 by Ramona Bass and Arnold Rampersad. Reprinted by permission of Hill and Wang, a division of Farrar, Straus and Giroux, LLC. and Harold Ober Associates Incorporated.

"The Circuit" by Francisco Jiménez, from *The Circuit*: *Stories from the Life of a Migrant Child*. Copyright © 1997 Francisco Jiménez. Reprinted by permission of University of New Mexico Press.

"The Last Leaf" by O. Henry, from *The Complete Works of O. Henry* by O. Henry. Published by Garden City books, a division of Bantam Doubleday Dell, Inc.

"The Lottery" by Shirley Jackson, from *The Lottery* by Shirley Jackson. Copyright © 1948, 1949 by Shirley Jackson. Copyright renewed 1976, 1977 by Laurence Hyman, Barry Hyman, Mrs. Sarah Webster and Mrs. Joanne Schnurer. Reprinted by permission of Farrar, Straus and Giroux, LLC. and Linda Allen Agency.

"The One Day War" by Judith Soloway. Copyright © 1985 by Judith Soloway. Reprinted by permission of the author.

"The Third Level" by Jack Finney. Reprinted by permission of Don Congdon Associates, Inc. Copyright © 1957, renewed 1985 by Jack Finney.

"All Summer in a Day" by Ray Bradbury. Reprinted by permission of Don Congdon Associates, Inc. Copyright © 1954 by the Mercury Press, renewed 1982 by Ray Bradbury.

"Désirée's Baby" by Kate Chopin, from *The Awakening and Selected Stories of Kate Chopin*, Barbara H. Solomon. 1976, New American Library, a division of Penguin USA.

"A Visit to Grandmother" by William Melvin Kelley, from *Dancers on the Shore*. Copyright © 1964 by William Melvin Kelley. Used by permission of William Morris Endeavor Entertainment, LLC, on behalf of the author.

"Too Soon a Woman" by Dorothy M. Johnson. Copyright © 1953 by Dorothy M. Johnson. Reprinted by permission of McIntosh & Otis, Inc. First appeared in *Cosmopolitan Magazine*, 1953.

"Thicker Than Water" by Ralph Henry Barbour and George Randolph Osborne. First published in 1916. Taken from *Flash Fiction Online*, June 2010 Issue (http://www.flashfictiononline.com/fpublic0037-thicker-than-water-ralph-henry-barbour-george-osborne.html).

The authors would like to thank the following reviewers for their thoughtful and useful feedback: Ann Abeyta, Austin Community College, Austin, Texas; Joseph Granitto, Long Island University, South Setauket, New York; Beth Haidt, Queens College, City University of New York, Flushing, New York; Patrice Plummer, California State University, Bakersfield, California; Kathy Smith, Saddleback College, Mission Viejo, California; and Juanita Villarreal, Universidad Regiomontana, Monterrey, Mexico.

INDEX